MARIAN GETZ SPENT HER CHILDHOOD AS THE DAUGHTER OF MISSIONARIES IN THE CONGO, AFRICA. SHE LEARNED HOW TO COOK BY READING HER MOTHER'S COOKBOOKS AND USING A CAST IRON WOOD BURNING STOVE. SHE OWNED HER OWN CATERING COMPANY IN KANSAS BEFORE BECOMING THE DISTRICT TRAINER FOR CAKE DECORATORS OF A MAJOR FLORIDA GROCERY STORE. A PASTRY CHEF FOR WOLFGANG PUCK SINCE 1998, MARIAN HAS BEEN FEATURED IN SEVERAL NATIONAL MAGAZINES AND WAS SELECTED BY HER PEERS AS ONE OF THE TOP 10 CHEFS IN CENTRAL FLORIDA. SHE HAS ALSO BEEN HONORED WITH THE "OUTSTANDING ACHIEVEMENT AWARD" IN 2007 FROM HER ALMA MATER, OTTAWA UNIVERSITY. MARIAN HAS TAKEN HER EXPERIENCE AS A PASTRY CHEF, WIFE, MOTHER, AND NOW GRANDMOTHER TO PUT TOGETHER A PIE MAKER COOKBOOK THAT WILL NOT ONLY SATISFY YOUR SWEET TOOTH BUT ALSO HELP YOU BECOME A BETTER CHEF IN THE KITCHEN. THIS COLLECTION OF AMAZING RECIPES, MOUTH WATERING PHOTOS, MARIAN'S HELPFUL STEP-BY-STEP TIPS AND RESOURCE PAGE WILL GIVE YOU A WHOLE NEW PERSPECTIVE ON COOKING MEALS AND DESSERTS THAT ARE DELICIOUS AND EASY TO PREPARE.

ACKNOWLEDGMENTS

A most sincere thank you to our wonderful viewers and customers for without you there would be no need for a cookbook. I try very hard to give you an array of recipes suited for the particular kitchen tool the cookbook is written for. Wolfgang and I create recipes faster than we can write them down. That is what chefs do and is also the reason to tune in to the live shows and even record them so you can learn new dishes that may not be in our cookbooks yet.

Thank you most of all to Wolfgang. You are the most passionate chef I know and it has been a privilege to work for you since 1998. You are a great leader and friend. Your restaurants are full of cooks and staff that have been with you for 20 or more years which is a true testament to how you lead us. Thanks for allowing me to write these cookbooks and for letting me share the stage at HSN with you.

To Greg, my sweet husband since 1983. Working together is a dream and I love you. You have taught me what a treasure it is to have a home filled with people to laugh with.

To my sons, Jordan and Benjamin, we have a beautiful life, don't we? It just keeps on getting better since we added Lindsay, J.J. and now precious Easton, our first grandbaby.

To all the great people at WP Productions, Syd, Arnie, Mike, Phoebe, Michael, Nicolle, Tracy, Genevieve, Gina, Craig, Nancy, Sylvain, Rodney and the rest of the team, you are all amazing to work with. Watching all the wonderful items we sell develop from idea to final product on live television is an awe-inspiring process to see and I love that I get to be a part of it.

To Daniel Koren, our patient editor and photographer, thank you for your dedication. You make the photo shoot days fun and you are such an easygoing person to work with in the cramped, hot studio we have to share. We have learned so much together and have far more to learn.

To Greg, Cat, Estela, Jimmy, Angi, Jen, Laurie and Tomasa who are the most dedicated, loving staff anyone could wish for. You are the true heroes behind the scenes. You are a well-oiled machine of very hard working people who pull off the live shows at HSN. It is a magical production to watch, from the first box unpacked, to the thousands of eggs cracked and beaten to running to get that "thing" Wolf asks for at the last minute, to the very last dish washed and put away it is quite a sight to behold. I love you all and I deeply love what we do.

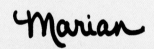

Whether I am preparing the food in my restaurants or enjoying an evening out, dessert is a must have treat to make a dining experience complete. I have a huge sweet tooth and dessert is something that I can't seem to skip. That's where the pie maker comes in. It is a small appliance that can have your dessert ready in no time.

When I asked Marian to write the cookbook for the pie maker, I knew she would rise to the occasion. Her experience as a pastry chef, wife, mother, and now a grandmother allowed Marian to put together a pie maker cookbook with a wide variety of recipes that I'm sure you will use for years to come.

A student of cooking is probably one of the best ways to describe Marian. She is always looking for something new, something fresh, something local, something seasonal. Her culinary knowledge combined with her passion for cooking is second to none. The recipes that Marian has written for the pie maker cookbook will motivate you to be more creative in the kitchen.

As I learned long ago, alongside my mother and grandmother, you should always put lots of love into everything you cook. This is certainly evident in this collection of Marian's pie maker recipes.

Wolfgang Puck

TABLE OF CONTENTS

GLUTEN-FREE

DOUGHS & TOPPINGS

PIE MAKER TIPS

Cooking Times

The suggested cooking times throughout this book assume that you first fill the pie maker with the desired crusts and fillings while the unit is unplugged. It was written this way to prevent any burns that may occur if you tried filling a preheated pie maker. The pie maker only takes a few minutes to heat up so there's no significant loss of time using it this way.

Pie Crusts

Premade store-bought pie dough is found usually in long boxes in the dairy section at the grocery store near the cookie dough. There are generally 2 pie dough rounds per box.

Puff pastry and phyllo dough packages are found in the freezer section near the dessert items and also come in a long box with 2 folded sheets per box.

You may be wondering why I think puff pastry is so great for top crusts? It is because when the pie maker is closed, the puff pastry puffs up and fills in any empty space, giving you a domed pie top that is perfectly browned.

If your pies ever come out with white, uncooked looking tops, carefully invert the latched-closed pie maker onto a folded kitchen towel for a few minutes. This allows gravity to help brown the pale top. Pale tops simply mean that not enough filling was added to create contact with the top lid.

Removing Baked Goods From The Pie Maker

Using aluminum foil strips in each pie mold will make it much easier for you to remove your pretty creations from the pie maker. I precut and keep a stash of them ready for use at all times. Cut the strips using scissors to measure 10" long by 2" wide. In the alternative, you can use a potholder and slightly invert the open pie maker over them to remove the baked goods. For open-faced tarts use a small spatula or bamboo skewer to aid you in removal.

*Cut "foil lifter" strips
10" long x 2" wide*

*Lay a foil strip over each pie mold
to aid with removal once baked*

Cutting Bottom Dough Crusts

You pie maker comes with a pie cutter that has a large side and a small side. Use the large side to cut bottom dough crusts as shown below and the small side to cut top crusts.

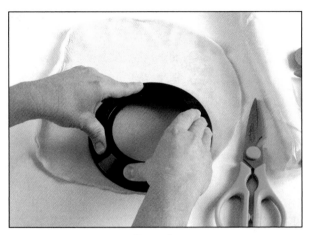

Step 1:
Use the large side of the pastry cutter to cut out pie bottom dough crusts

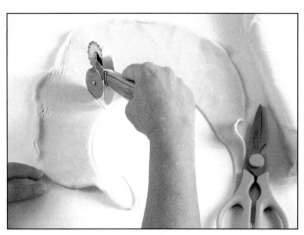

Step 2:
Trim one side of excess dough

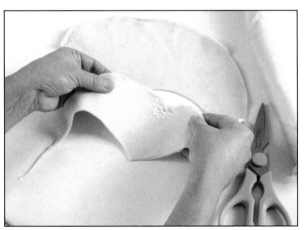

Step 3:
Place trimmed dough piece on remaining dough

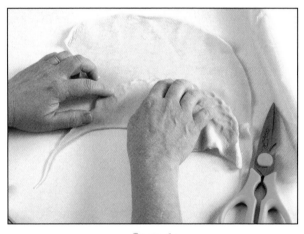

Step 4:
Using your fingers, press the ends together to seal

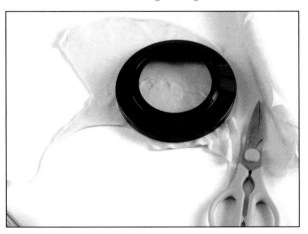

Step 5:
Cut out another bottom crust from the patched dough

Top Crusts:
Use the small side of the pie cutter to cut out puff pastry top crusts

PIE MAKER TIPS

Using Dough Scraps

Don't waste the dough after cutting out pie dough bottoms and puff pastry tops. Use cookie cutters of your choice or a pastry/pizza wheel to cut out fun shapes to decorate your pies. They do not need to be egg washed to stick to the top crust so just lay them on top and they will seal to the dough's surface when you close the pie maker. Kids love to have their name's first initial or a number cut out matching their age.

Use cookie cutters or a pastry wheel to cut out decorative pieces

You can make many different shapes to decorate your pies

Using Other Doughs

For lazy days, I use plain bread as crusts for mini pizzas or pies. Tortillas or patted out biscuit dough also work well. You can buy empanada dough in small and large sizes in the freezer section of Latin markets that make cutting out dough unnecessary. They don't puff up and brown as well as puff pastry but they sure are easy and convenient.

Storing Crusts

I like to cut out many top and bottom pie crusts and place them between sheets of parchment paper. I place them in a large zipper top bag and put them in the freezer. That way I always have crusts on hand and can create pies in a snap.

Cupcake Liners

If you prefer, you can use cupcake liners in the pie molds. I often do because I like how they add a finished touch to the cupcakes. They also act as a napkin when serving. The jumbo or large style muffin and cupcake liners work best in this pie maker.

Loading The Bottom Crust In The Pie Maker

Below is a step by step guide on how to load your bottom crust into your pie maker using the foil lifters to aid you in removal once baked.

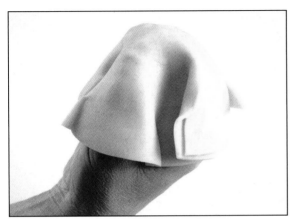

Step 1:
*Drape the bottom pie dough
over your fingers*

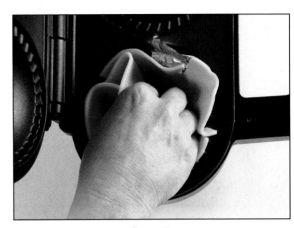

Step 2:
*Place bottom crust over the foil strip into
the pie mold*

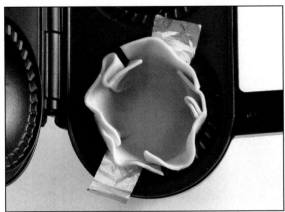

Step 3:
*Gently ease in by lifting the edges and
pressing the center*

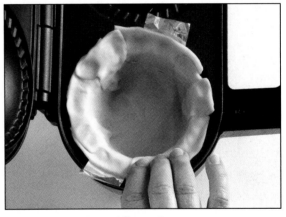

Step 4:
*Press the top edge of the crust into the
grooved perimeter*

Step 5:
*Add 3/4 - 1 cup of filling then cover with
top crust and any decorative pieces*

Step 6:
*When baking is complete, lift the pie by the
foil strip to remove from the pie maker*

PIE MAKER TIPS

Capacity

The Wolfgang Puck pie maker wells hold about 3/4 - 1 cup of filling. Other brands have shallower wells and in general hold approximately 1/3 cup of filling.

Baking

There are 3 main things that you need to do each time you bake to get great results:

1.   Measure accurately every time
2.   Have good equipment, even if it is basic
3.   Set a timer, the kind that can travel with you from room to room

The most important thing in baking is accurate measuring. Use glass measuring cups to measure liquid ingredients. Use metal measuring cups for dry ingredients. Measuring spoons are best if they are narrow enough to fit into the neck of a spice jar.

Be Organized

Read through the recipe once then gather all the ingredients before you start to measure the ingredients and start to bake.

Measuring In Piles

Try to keep the dry ingredients as separate as possible when first adding them to the mixing bowl. For example, add the flour in a pile on one side of the mixing bowl then add the sugar in a separate pile, add the baking powder in another pile then do the same thing for the rest of the ingredients. By doing this, you will be able to read over the ingredients again if you ever get distracted which happens to all of us. So many people give up baking because they make a mistake in measuring which results in the finished baked goods not turning out properly. This will help you retrace your steps if necessary and ensure proper measuring of ingredients.

Use Caution

Use caution when dealing with hot baked goods as they can produce burns if not handled correctly. Keep a pair of hand mitts or potholders nearby.

Testing For Doneness

To test for doneness, with cakes, insert a wooden pick or bamboo skewer off-center. It should generally come out with just a few moist crumbs clinging to it. For custards, insert a knife off-center and it should come out clean. For breads, bake until the internal temperature registers 200°F on a thermometer. For pizzas and pastries look for slight puffing and a brown color.

Vanilla

I adore vanilla and order both my vanilla extract and vanilla beans from a supplier directly from the island of Tahiti. I use both of these in recipes where the vanilla flavor takes center stage. In recipes where vanilla is not the star flavor, I use imitation vanilla because it is less expensive and adds the right amount of taste and aroma without overpowering the other flavors. My favorite is an inexpensive imitation flavoring called Magic Line Butter Vanilla Extract. It adds an incredible sweet smell and taste to baked goods.

Chocolate

Buy good quality chocolate and cocoa whenever possible. It is easy to find excellent chocolate at most grocery stores but it is almost impossible to find good quality cocoa powder. I suggest ordering it online.

Butter

All of the butter used in this book is unsalted. Softened butter means butter that has been left at room temperature for several hours. It should be soft enough to offer no resistance whatsoever when sliced using a knife. While there is no perfect substitute for the pure flavor of butter, you can use a substitute such as margarine and most of the recipes will turn out fairly well.

Salt

The salt used in this book is Diamond Crystal Kosher Salt. It is half as salty as most other brands. This is because the grains are very fluffy and therefore not as many fit into a measuring spoon. This brand also lists only "salt" as the ingredient on the box. If you are using salt other than Diamond Crystal Kosher Salt, simply use half the amount specified in the recipe.

Sugar Substitute

If you need to use a sugar substitute, my favorite kind is an all-natural product called Zsweet. I get it at my local health food store. While it does not bake as perfectly as regular sugar, it is the best substitute I know.

BBQ CHICKEN PIE

Makes 2 servings

Ingredients:

2 bottom crusts, store-bought or use recipe on page 95
2 top crusts, cut from store-bought puff pastry
1 pound roast chicken, chopped
1/4 cup bottled BBQ sauce
1/2 cup sautéed onions
Kosher salt and fresh pepper to taste

Method:

1. *Cut out top and bottom pie crusts using the pastry cutter.*
2. *In a bowl, combine the chicken, BBQ sauce, onions, salt and pepper.*
3. *Lay a foil strip over each pie mold to aid with removal once baked.*
4. *Place bottom crusts over foil strips into the pie molds then gently ease in by lifting the edges and pressing the centers.*
5. *Press the top edge of each crust into the grooved perimeter.*
6. *Divide the chicken between the pie molds then cover with top crusts; close and latch the lid.*
7. *Plug in the pie maker and bake for 10-12 minutes or until desired doneness.*
8. *When baking is complete, lift the pockets by the foil strips to remove from the pie maker and serve.*

CHICKEN POT PIE

Makes 2 servings

Ingredients:

1 tablespoon canola oil

6 boneless, skinless chicken thighs

Kosher salt and fresh pepper to taste

1 large yellow onion, peeled and diced

3 large carrots, peeled and diced

3 celery stalks, diced

2 large Russet potatoes, peeled and cubed

3 bay leaves

4 cups chicken stock

1/2 cup half & half + plus more for brushing

1/4 cup all purpose flour

1/2 cup milk

1 cup frozen peas

2 bottom pie crusts, store-bought or use recipe on page 95

2 top crusts, cut from store-bought puff pastry

Assorted Fresh Herbs (optional)

Method:

1. *Heat the oil in a large saucepan over medium-high heat.*
2. *Pat chicken dry using paper towels then season with salt and pepper.*
3. *When oil is hot, add the chicken to the saucepan and brown on both sides.*
4. *Add the onions, carrots, and celery; cook for 5 minutes, stirring often.*
5. *Add the potatoes, bay leaves, stock, and half & half; season with salt and pepper to taste then simmer for 1 hour.*
6. *In a bowl, combine the flour and milk; whisk the flour mixture into the chicken mixture to thicken.*
7. *Turn off the heat then stir in the peas; taste and adjust seasoning if desired.*
8. *Lay a foil strip over each pie mold to aid with removal once baked.*
9. *Cut out top and bottom pie crusts using the pastry cutter.*
10. *Place bottom crusts over the foil strips into the pie molds then gently ease in by lifting the edges and pressing the centers.*
11. *Press the top edge of each crust into the grooved perimeter.*
12. *Fill each pie mold with chicken mixture until slightly mounded above the rim.*
13. *Cover with top crusts and press fresh herbs onto the crusts if desired; close and latch the lid.*
14. *Plug in the pie maker and bake for 12-15 minutes or until desired doneness.*
15. *When baking is complete, lift the pies by the foil strips to remove from the pie maker and serve.*

AMERICAN
TACO PIE

Makes 2 servings

Ingredients:

2 flour tortillas

1/2 cup prepared refried beans or black beans

1 cup ground beef or chicken, cooked and crumbled

1/4 cup prepared salsa

1/2 cup Monterrey Jack cheese, shredded

1/4 cup white onions, diced

1/4 teaspoon ground cumin

Kosher salt and fresh pepper to taste

Method:

1. *Using the large side of the pastry cutter, trim the flour tortillas to fit the bottom crust if necessary.*

2. *Place a foil strip over each pie mold to aid with removal once baked.*

3. *Press a flour tortilla over the foil strip into each pie mold (use a drinking glass to help fit it into the pie mold).*

4. *Divide remaining ingredients between the pie molds in the order listed, mounding each slightly above the rim; close and latch the lid.*

5. *Plug in the pie maker and bake for 15 minutes or until browned.*

6. *When baking is complete, lift the pies by the foil strips to remove from the pie maker.*

7. *Garnish as desired and serve immediately.*

14

TURKEY POT PIE

Makes 2 servings

Ingredients:

1 tablespoon canola oil

1 large yellow onion, peeled and diced

3 large carrots, peeled and diced

3 celery stalks, diced

2 large Russet potatoes, peeled and cubed

3 bay leaves

1 teaspoon dried sage

1 pound roast turkey, cooked and chopped

4 cups chicken stock

1/2 cup half & half

Kosher salt and fresh pepper to taste

1/4 cup all purpose flour

1/2 cup milk

1/2 cup peas, frozen

2 bottom crusts, store-bought or use recipe on page 95

2 top crusts, cut from store-bought puff pastry

Method:

1. *Heat oil in a large sauce pan over medium heat.*

2. *When oil is hot, add the onions, carrots, celery, potatoes, bay leaves and sage; cook for 5 minutes.*

3. *Add the turkey, stock and half & half; season with salt and pepper then simmer for 1 hour.*

4. *In a bowl, combine the flour and milk; whisk flour mixture into the turkey mixture to thicken.*

5. *Turn off the heat then stir in the peas; taste and adjust seasoning if desired.*

6. *Lay a foil strip over each pie mold to aid with removal once baked.*

7. *Cut out top and bottom pie crusts using the pastry cutter.*

8. *Place bottom crusts over foil strips into the pie molds then gently ease in by lifting the edges and pressing the centers.*

9. *Press the top edge of each crust into the grooved perimeter.*

10. *Fill pie molds with turkey mixture to the top.*

11. *Cover with top crusts; close and latch the lid.*

12. *Plug in the pie maker and bake for 12-15 minutes or until desired doneness.*

13. *When baking is complete, lift the pies by the foil strips to remove from the pie maker and serve.*

CHEESY RIGATONI WITH TOMATO SAUCE

Makes 2 servings

Ingredients:

1 3/4 cups rigatoni pasta, cooked

2 tablespoons whole milk ricotta cheese

1 large egg

1/4 cup Parmesan cheese, grated

1/3 cup mozzarella cheese, shredded

1 garlic clove, minced

2 teaspoons flat leaf parsley, chopped

Pinch of chili flakes

Kosher salt and fresh pepper to taste

1/3 cup warmed marinara sauce, for serving

Method:

1. *In a bowl, combine all ingredients, except marinara sauce; stir to combine.*
2. *Lay a foil strip over each pie mold to aid with removal once baked.*
3. *Divide the pasta mixture evenly between the pie molds, mounding slightly above the rims; close and latch the lid.*
4. *Plug in the pie maker and cook for 10 minutes or until well browned.*
5. *When cooking is complete, lift the pasta by the foil strips to remove from the pie maker.*
6. *Transfer to small plates then pour some marinara around each pasta bake.*
7. *Garnish as desired and serve hot.*

BROCCOLI & HAM
QUICHE

Makes 2 servings

Ingredients:

2 bottom crusts, store-bought or see recipe page 95
4 large eggs
1/4 cup ham, diced
1/4 cup broccoli florets, cooked
1 green onion, chopped
1/4 cup Swiss cheese, grated
Kosher salt and fresh pepper to taste

Method:

1. *Lay a foil strip over each pie mold to aid with removal once baked.*
2. *Cut out 2 bottom pie crusts using the large side of the pastry cutter.*
3. *Place the bottom crusts over the foil strips into the pie molds then gently ease in by lifting the edges and pressing the centers.*
4. *Press the top edge of each crust into the grooved perimeter.*
5. *In a bowl, beat the eggs until incorporated.*
6. *Stir in remaining ingredients.*
7. *Divide the mixture between the pie molds until almost full; close and latch the lid.*
8. *Plug in the pie maker and bake for 12-15 minutes or until the filling is just set.*
9. *When baking is complete, lift the quiche by the foil strips to remove from the pie maker.*
10. *Garnish as desired before serving.*

EASY
SAMOSAS

Makes 2 servings

Ingredients:

2 teaspoons unsalted butter

8 ounces ground beef or lamb

1 medium yellow onion, diced

2 garlic cloves, minced

1-inch piece of fresh ginger, minced

1/2 teaspoon apple cider vinegar

2 teaspoons powdered chicken bouillon, such as Maggi

1 tablespoon curry powder

1/2 cup frozen peas, thawed

2 phyllo bottom crusts (see recipe on page 96)

2 phyllo top crusts (see recipe on page 96)

Method:

1. *In a large saucepan over medium heat, melt the butter.*
2. *Add the beef, onions, garlic, ginger and vinegar; cook until the meat is cooked through and onions are tender.*
3. *Add the bouillon and curry powder; stir to combine.*
4. *Add the peas and gently stir to combine; remove from heat.*
5. *Cut out top and bottom crusts using the pastry cutter.*
6. *Lay a foil strip over each pie mold to aid with removal once baked.*
7. *Place bottom crusts over the foil strips into the pie molds then gently ease in by lifting the edges and pressing the centers.*
8. *Press the top edge of each crust into the grooved perimeter.*
9. *Spoon mixture into each pie mold until slightly mounded above the rim.*
10. *Cover with top crusts; close and latch the lid.*
11. *Plug in the pie maker and cook for 12-15 minutes or until browned.*
12. *When baking is complete, lift the samosas by the foil strips to remove from the pie maker and serve.*

SPINACH FETA PIE

Makes 2 servings

Ingredients:

1 pound frozen spinach, thawed and drained

1/2 cup heavy cream

1/4 cup green onions, chopped

Kosher salt and fresh pepper to taste

1/4 teaspoon crushed red pepper flakes (optional)

1 cup feta cheese, crumbled and divided

2 bottom crusts, store-bought or see recipe on page 95

2 top crusts, cut from store-bought puff pastry

Method:

1. *In a mixing bowl, combine the spinach, cream, onions, salt, pepper, red pepper flakes (if desired) and 3/4 cup feta cheese.*
2. *Lay a foil strip over each pie mold to aid with removal once baked.*
3. *Cut out bottom and top crusts using the pastry cutter.*
4. *Place bottom crusts over the foil strips into the pie molds then gently ease in by lifting the edges and pressing the centers.*
5. *Press the top edge of each crust into the grooved perimeter.*
6. *Divide the spinach filling between the pie molds.*
7. *Top each with remaining feta cheese then cover with top crusts; close and latch the lid.*
8. *Plug in the pie maker and bake for 12-15 minutes or until browned.*
9. *When baking is complete, lift the pies by the foil strips to remove from the pie maker.*
10. *Garnish as desired and serve.*

CRISPY TUNA CASSEROLE PIE

Makes 2 servings

Ingredients:

1 cup leftover mashed potatoes

1/2 cup home made onion rings or canned French fried onion rings

1 can (5.5 ounces) tuna fish, drained

1 large egg

2 green onions, chopped

1 celery stalk, chopped

2 tablespoons Parmesan cheese

2 bottom crusts, store-bought or see recipe on page 95

2 top crusts, cut from store-bought puff pastry

Method:

1. *In a bowl, combine all ingredients, except crusts; mix well.*
2. *Cut out top and bottom pie crusts using the pastry cutter.*
3. *Lay a foil strip over each pie mold to aid with removal once baked and press in using a spatula.*
4. *Place bottom crusts over the foil strips into the pie molds then gently ease in by lifting the edges and pressing the centers.*
5. *Press the top edge of each crust into the grooved perimeter.*
6. *Spoon tuna mixture into each pie mold until mounded slightly above the rim.*
7. *Cover with top crusts; close and latch the lid.*
8. *Plug in the pie maker and cook for 10-12 minutes or until browned.*
9. *When cooking is complete, lift the pies by the foil strips to remove from the pie maker.*
10. *Garnish as desired and serve.*

TIP

This is a great way to use up leftovers as you can substitute the tuna for ham, leftover cooked ground beef, turkey, tofu or more vegetables.

MY FAVORITE
TURKEY BURGERS

Makes 2 burgers

For the Burgers:

6 ounces lean ground turkey

2 tablespoons ricotta cheese

1 tablespoon yellow onion, minced

1 tablespoon celery, minced

1/4 teaspoon dried sage

Kosher salt and fresh pepper to taste

For Serving:

Small soft buns

Cheddar cheese slices

Tomato slices

Red onion slices

Pickle slices

Bib lettuce

Method:

1. *In a bowl, combine all burger ingredients then form the mixture into 2 patties.*

2. *Place a patty into each pie mold; close and latch the lid.*

3. *Plug in the pie maker and cook for 5 minutes then open the lid and flip each patty over using a small spatula.*

4. *Close and latch the lid again then cook for an additional 2-3 minutes or until internal temperature of the patties registers 165°F on a meat thermometer.*

5. *Remove and serve on buns with desired toppings.*

EASY GLAZED
MEATLOAF MINIS

Makes 2 servings

For the Meatloaf:

1 white bread slice, cubed
1 tablespoon whole milk
10 ounces lean ground beef
1 small yellow onion, finely chopped
1 large egg, beaten
1/4 teaspoon kosher salt or to taste
1/2 teaspoon freshly cracked pepper
1 tablespoon ketchup
1 tablespoon yellow mustard

For the Glaze:

1 tablespoon yellow mustard
1/4 cup ketchup
1 tablespoon light brown sugar, packed

Method:

1. *In a bowl, combine the bread cubes and milk.*
2. *Add remaining meatloaf ingredients; mix gently together.*
3. *Divide the mixture in half then shape each portion into a ball.*
4. *Lay a foil strip over each pie mold to aid with removal once cooked.*
5. *Place a meatloaf ball over the foil strip into each pie mold; close and latch the lid.*
6. *Plug in the pie maker and cook for 5 minutes then open and flip meatloaves over.*
7. *Close and latch the lid again and cook for an additional 5 minutes or until internal temperature or the meatloaves register 165°F degrees on a meat thermometer.*
8. *When cooking is complete, lift the meatloaves by the foil strips to remove from the pie maker.*
9. *To make the glaze, combine all glaze ingredients in a microwave-safe bowl; microwave until hot.*
10. *Pour hot glaze over the meatloaves, garnish as desired and serve.*

BEEF POT PIE

Makes 2 servings

Ingredients:

1 tablespoon unsalted butter

1/4 cup yellow onions, diced

1 tablespoon all purpose flour

Kosher salt and fresh pepper to taste

2/3 cup beef stock

1/2 cup potatoes, boiled and cubed

1/2 cup frozen mixed vegetables, thawed

1/2 cup roast beef, cooked and diced

2 bottom crusts, store-bought or use recipe on page 95

2 top crusts, cut from store-bought puff pastry

Method:

1. *Melt the butter in a large saucepan over medium heat.*
2. *Add the onions and cook for 2 minutes.*
3. *Use a whisk to mix in the flour, salt and pepper.*
4. *Gradually add the stock and stir until thickened.*
5. *Add the potatoes, vegetables and beef then stir until heated through; remove from heat.*
6. *Cut out top and bottom crusts using the pastry cutter.*
7. *Lay a foil strip over each pie mold to aid with removal once baked.*
8. *Place bottom crusts over foil strips into the pie molds then gently ease in by lifting the edges and pressing the centers.*
9. *Press the top edge of each crust into the grooved perimeter.*
10. *Pour beef mixture into each pie mold until slightly mounded above the rim.*
11. *Cover with top crusts; close and latch the lid.*
12. *Plug in the pie maker and bake for 10-12 minutes or until desired doneness.*
13. *When baking is complete, lift the pies by the foil strips to remove from the pie maker and serve.*

SHEPHERD'S PIE

Makes 4 servings

Ingredients:

1 pound ground beef

1 tablespoon beef bouillon, such as Maggi

Kosher salt and fresh pepper to taste

1/2 yellow onion, chopped

2 tablespoons all purpose flour

1 cup frozen mixed vegetables, thawed

2 bottom crusts, store-bought or use recipe on page 95

2 cups mashed potatoes, hot, divided

Method:

1. *In a sauce pan over medium heat, brown the ground beef.*
2. *Add the bouillon, salt, pepper, and onions; cook for 5 minutes.*
3. *Add the flour and stir to combine.*
4. *Remove from heat.*
5. *Add the vegetables and gently stir to combine.*
6. *Cut out 2 bottom pie crusts using the large side of the pastry cutter.*
7. *Lay a foil strip over each pie mold to aid with removal once baked.*
8. *Place bottom crusts over foil strips into the pie molds then gently ease in by lifting the edges and pressing the centers.*
9. *Press the top edge of each crust into the grooved perimeter.*
10. *Fill each pie mold with beef mixture until 3/4 full; close and latch the lid.*
11. *Plug in the pie maker and bake for 12-15 minutes or until crust is browned.*
12. *When baking is complete, lift the pies by the foil strips to remove from the pie maker.*
13. *Top with mashed potatoes, garnish as desired and serve.*

ZUCCHINI & BACON QUICHE

Makes 2 servings

Ingredients:

2 bottom crusts, store-bought or see recipe on page 95
4 large eggs
4 bacon strips, cooked and crumbled
1/4 cup fresh zucchini, squeezed dry and grated
1 green onion, chopped
1 tablespoon Parmesan cheese, grated
1/4 cup Swiss cheese, grated
Kosher salt and fresh pepper to taste

Method:

1. *Cut out 2 bottom pie crusts using the large side of the pastry cutter.*
2. *Lay a foil strip over each pie mold to aid with removal once baked.*
3. *Place bottom crusts over foil strips into the pie molds then gently ease in by lifting the edges and pressing the centers.*
4. *Press the top edge of each crust into the grooved perimeter.*
5. *In a mixing bowl, beat the eggs until incorporated then stir in remaining ingredients.*
6. *Fill the pie molds to the top with zucchini mixture; close and latch the lid.*
7. *Plug in the pie maker and bake for 12-15 minutes or until filling is just set.*
8. *When baking is complete, lift quiche by the foil strips to remove from the pie maker.*
9. *Garnish as desired and serve.*

CAPRESE
TART

Makes 2 servings

Ingredients:

2 bottom crusts, store-bought or see recipe on page 95
12 cherry tomatoes, halved
12 small mozzarella cheese balls
1 tablespoon olive oil
1 tablespoon balsamic vinegar
1 large basil leaf, julienned
Kosher salt and fresh pepper to taste

Method:

1. *Lay a foil strip over each pie mold to aid with removal once baked.*
2. *Cut out 2 bottom pie crusts using the large side of the pastry cutter.*
3. *Place bottom crusts over foil strips into the pie molds then gently ease in by lifting the edges and pressing the centers.*
4. *Press the top edge of each crust into the grooved perimeter; close and latch the lid.*
5. *Plug in the pie maker and bake crusts only for about 12 minutes or until desired doneness.*
6. *When baking is complete, lift the crusts by the foil strips to remove from the pie maker.*
7. *In a bowl, combine the tomatoes, cheese balls, oil, and vinegar; toss to combine.*
8. *Divide the tomato mixture evenly between the crusts.*
9. *Drizzle tops with additional vinegar and garnish with basil.*
10. *Sprinkle with salt and pepper and serve.*

ANTIPASTO
TART

Makes 4 servings

Ingredients:

4 bottom crusts, store-bought or see recipe on page 95

8 ounces hard salami, thinly sliced, rolled, chilled and divided

12 green olives, divided

12 black olives, divided

12 grape tomatoes, divided

16 small mozzarella cheese balls, divided

2 tablespoons olive oil, divided

2 tablespoons balsamic vinegar, divided

2 large basil leaves, julienned

Kosher salt and fresh pepper to taste

Method:

1. *Lay a foil strip over each pie mold to aid with removal once baked.*
2. *Cut out 4 bottom crusts using the large side of the pastry cutter.*
3. *Place bottom crusts over foil strips into the pie molds then gently ease in by lifting the edges and pressing the centers.*
4. *Press the top edge of each crust into the grooved perimeter.*
5. *Close and latch the lid; bake crust only for about 12 minutes or until desired doneness.*
6. *When baking is complete, lift the crusts by the foil strips to remove from the pie maker and repeat to make additional crusts if needed.*
7. *Divide the salami, olives, tomatoes and cheese into 4 portions.*
8. *Fill each baked crust with salami, olives, tomatoes and cheese in a decorative pattern.*
9. *Drizzle 1/2 tablespoon of olive oil and 1/2 tablespoon balsamic vinegar over each tart.*
10. *Top with basil then sprinkle with salt and pepper before serving.*

MAC & CHEESE

Makes 2 servings

Ingredients:

1/2 cup half & half
2 tablespoons Parmesan cheese, grated
2 tablespoons mozzarella cheese, grated
2 tablespoons Cheddar cheese, grated
1 teaspoon powdered bouillon, such as Maggi
2 cups elbow macaroni, cooked

Method:

1. *In a microwave-safe bowl, combine the half & half, cheeses and bouillon.*
2. *Microwave for 1 minute then remove and stir well.*
3. *Microwave for an additional 1 minute or until hot; stir until smooth.*
4. *Add the macaroni to the cheese mixture; stir to combine.*
5. *Divide the mixture between the pie molds; close and latch the lid.*
6. *Plug in the pie maker and cook for 12-15 minutes or until browned.*
7. *Remove and serve warm.*

TIP

You can use leftover mac & cheese for this recipe. If
you're in a time crunch, use the pre-made mac & cheese
available at the grocery store.

28

EASY SANDWICH
BREAD PIZZAS

Makes 2 servings

Ingredients:

2 white or wheat sandwich bread slices

1 tablespoon prepared marinara sauce, divided

4 pepperoni slices

2 tablespoons mozzarella cheese, shredded and divided

Method:

1. *Lay a foil strip over each pie mold to aid with removal once baked.*
2. *Push a bread slice over each foil strip into each pie mold.*
3. *Top each bread slice with 1/2 tablespoon marinara sauce, 2 pepperoni slices and 1 tablespoon mozzarella cheese; close and latch the lid.*
4. *Plug in the pie maker and cook for 15 minutes or until browned.*
5. *When cooking is complete, lift the pizzas by the foil strips to remove from the pie maker.*
6. *Serve immediately.*

TIP

You can bake the bread slices without any toppings for 8-10 minutes, then remove and top with peanut butter and jelly or peanut butter and banana. My grandson loves these little snacks.

PEPPERONI PIZZA PIE

Makes 2 servings

Ingredients:

8 ounces store-bought pizza dough
4 tablespoons prepared marinara sauce
1 cup mozzarella cheese, shredded
2 tablespoons Parmesan cheese, grated
1 package (8 ounces) pepperoni slices
Kosher salt and fresh pepper to taste

Method:

1. *On a floured surface, roll out the pizza dough until 1/4-inch thick (if dough resists rolling, cover with a kitchen towel and let it rest for 10 minutes before rolling).*
2. *Cut out 2 bottom crusts and 2 top crusts from the pizza dough using the pastry cutter.*
3. *Lay a foil strip over each pie mold to aid with removal once baked.*
4. *Place bottom crusts over foil strips into the pie molds then gently ease in by lifting the edges and pressing the centers.*
5. *Press the top edge of each crust into the grooved perimeter.*
6. *Divide remaining ingredients between the pie molds in the order listed until slightly mounded above the rim of each pie mold (you may not need all of the pepperoni).*
7. *Cover with top crusts; close and latch the lid.*
8. *Plug in the pie maker and bake for 10-12 minutes or until well browned.*
9. *When baking is complete, lift the pizza pies by the foil strips to remove from the pie maker and serve.*

SAGE & RED ONION FOCACCIA

Makes 4 focaccia breads

For the Dough:

1/2 cup + 2 tablespoons water
1 package dry active yeast
1 tablespoon honey
1 1/2 cups all purpose flour
1 teaspoon kosher salt
1 tablespoon extra-virgin olive oil

For the Topping:

2 tablespoons extra-virgin olive oil, divided
1 teaspoon kosher salt, or to taste
4 fresh sage leaves, torn
4 thin red onion slices

Method:

1. *In a large bowl, combine all dough ingredients.*
2. *Using a wooden spoon, thoroughly mix until a smooth, wet dough forms.*
3. *Let dough stand for 10 minutes then mix again for 1 minute.*
4. *Pour half of the olive oil for the topping onto a small sheet pan and spread it around.*
5. *Pour and scrape the dough onto the sheet pan and top with remaining olive oil.*
6. *Pat and pull the dough into a square then divide the square into 4 pieces.*
7. *Let dough rest for 30 minutes.*
8. *Dimple dough all over using your finger tips then let rest for 5 minutes.*
9. *Sprinkle dough with the salt, sage and onions.*
10. *Drop a piece of dough into each pie mold; close but do not latch the lid.*
11. *Plug in the pie maker and bake for 10 minutes or until puffed and well browned.*
12. *Remove using a fork and repeat with remaining dough if desired.*
13. *Serve hot.*

TIP

If you are busy you can buy store-bought pizza dough at the grocery store and make this delicious bread in just a few minutes.

BREAKFAST ON THE GO
BISCUITS

Makes 4 servings

For the Biscuits:

3/4 cup all purpose flour
1 teaspoon sugar
1 teaspoon baking powder
1/2 teaspoon kosher salt
1/2 cup heavy cream

For the Toppings:

Bacon
Fried Egg
Jelly
Sausage patty
Canadian bacon
Peanut butter
Scrambled eggs
Cheese slices

Method:

1. *In a mixing bowl, combine all biscuit ingredients; stir until a dough ball forms.*
2. *Lay a foil strip over each pie mold to aid with removal once baked.*
3. *Divide the dough in half then place into each pie mold; close and latch the lid.*
4. *Plug in the pie maker and bake for 14-16 minutes or until browned and cooked through.*
5. *When baking is complete, lift the biscuits by the foil strips to remove from the pie maker.*
6. *Cut biscuits in half, add your favorite topping and enjoy your breakfast on the go.*

EASIEST FRIED
EGGS

Makes 2 servings

Ingredients:

2 teaspoons unsalted butter
4 large eggs
Kosher salt and fresh pepper to taste

Method:

1. *Plug in the pie maker.*
2. *Place 1 teaspoon butter into each pie mold and let it melt.*
3. *Carefully crack 2 eggs into each pie mold.*
4. *Season with salt and pepper; close and latch the lid.*
5. *Cook for 2 minutes to achieve a runny yolk, 3 minutes for a medium yolk or 4 minutes for a firm yolk.*
6. *Use a small spatula to lift the eggs out of pie maker.*
7. *Serve immediately.*

TIP

For scrambled eggs, beat 2 eggs for each pie mold, season to taste with salt and pepper, then pour into each pie mold once the butter has melted. Use a silicone spatula to stir the eggs gently as they cook and remove when eggs are just set but still glossy.

BACON & EGG BISCUIT CUPS

Makes 2 servings

Ingredients:

3/4 cup all purpose flour
1 teaspoon sugar
1 teaspoon baking powder
1/2 teaspoon kosher salt
1/2 cup heavy cream
1/4 cup bacon pieces, cooked
1/4 cup Cheddar cheese, shredded
2 large eggs

Method:

1. *In a bowl, combine the flour, sugar, baking powder, salt and cream; stir until a dough ball forms.*
2. *Lay a foil strip over each pie mold to aid with removal once baked.*
3. *Divide the dough between the pie molds over the foil strips then shape the dough into cups inside the pie molds.*
4. *Sprinkle bacon and cheese into each pie mold.*
5. *Crack an egg into each pie mold; close and latch the lid.*
6. *Plug in the pie maker and bake for 5-10 minutes or until biscuits are browned and eggs are cooked to desired doneness.*
7. *When baking is complete, lift the biscuits by the foil strips to remove from the pie maker.*
8. *Garnish as desired and serve.*

CORNY
CORNBREAD

Makes 2 servings

Ingredients:

1/2 cup unsalted butter, softened
3 large eggs
1/3 cup granulated sugar
1/2 cup plain yogurt, preferably Greek
1 cup corn, fresh, frozen or canned
1 tablespoon baking powder
2 teaspoon kosher salt
1/2 cup corn meal
1 1/2 cups unbleached all purpose flour

Method:

1. *Lay a foil strip over each pie mold to aid with removal once baked.*
2. *In a large bowl, combine all ingredients; mix well.*
3. *Fill each pie mold with batter until 3/4 full; close and latch the lid.*
4. *Plug in the pie maker and bake for 10-12 minutes or until a wooden pick inserted off-center comes out clean. If the pick is still wet from batter, cook for an additional 3-5 minutes.*
5. *When baking is complete, lift the cornbread by the foil strips to remove from the pie maker and serve.*

TIP
The batter will keep refrigerated in an airtight container for up to 3 days or in the freezer for up to 3 months.

BOSTON CREAM PIE

Makes 4 servings

For the Pies:

3/4 cup unsalted butter, softened
1 1/2 cups granulated sugar
3 large eggs
2 teaspoons pure vanilla extract
3/4 cup whole milk
2 cups unbleached all purpose flour
1/2 teaspoon kosher salt
2 teaspoons baking powder

For the Vanilla Pudding Filling:

3 tablespoons cornstarch
1/2 cup granulated sugar
2 cups half & half
1/8 teaspoon kosher salt
2 teaspoons pure vanilla extract
1/2 vanilla bean, split and seeds scraped out (see source page 106)

For Topping:

Chocolate Ganache (see recipe on page 101)

Method:

1. *In a bowl, cream the butter and sugar together using a spoon until well blended.*
2. *Mix in the eggs then add remaining pie ingredients and mix until a smooth batter forms.*
3. *Lay a foil strip over each pie mold to aid with removal once baked.*
4. *Pour batter into each pie mold until 1/2 full; close and latch the lid.*
5. *Plug in the pie maker and bake for 8 minutes or until golden brown.*
6. *While baking, prepare the pudding filling by whisking together all filling ingredients in a microwave-safe bowl; microwave for 6 minutes or until mixture boils.*
7. *Carefully remove filling, whisk for 30 seconds then microwave again for 2 minutes or until a full boil forms again.*
8. *Remove and cover while mixture cools to prevent a skin from forming on the surface.*
9. *When baking is complete, lift the pies by the foil strips to remove from the pie maker and let cool.*
10. *Cut each pie in half horizontally then fill each with 2 tablespoons of vanilla filling; replace the tops.*
11. *Spoon some chocolate ganache over the tops before serving.*

BANANA CREAM PIE

Makes 2 servings

Ingredients:

2 bottom crusts, store-bought or see recipe on page 95
1 1/2 cups whole milk
1/3 cup granulated sugar
2 tablespoons all purpose flour
Pinch of kosher salt
2 egg yolks, slightly beaten
1 tablespoons unsalted butter
1/2 teaspoon vanilla
1 banana + more for garnish

Method:

1. *Lay a foil strip over each pie mold to aid with removal once baked.*
2. *Cut out 2 bottom pie crusts using the large side of the pastry cutter.*
3. *Place bottom crusts over foil strips into the pie molds then gently ease in by lifting the edges and pressing the centers.*
4. *Press the top edge of each crust into the grooved perimeter.*
5. *Close and latch the lid; bake crust only for about 12 minutes or until desired doneness.*
6. *When baking is complete, lift the crusts by the foil strips to remove from the pie maker; set aside.*
7. *In a large saucepan over medium-high heat, bring the milk just to a simmer.*
8. *In another saucepan over medium-high heat, combine the sugar, flour and salt; gradually stir in the hot milk; stir constantly for about 2 minutes until thickened.*
9. *Pour egg yolks into a small bowl; stir a small amount of the hot mixture into the yolks; when combined, stir the yolks back into the remaining hot mixture.*
10. *Cook for 1 additional minute, stirring constantly.*
11. *Remove from heat, mix in the butter and vanilla then let rest until lukewarm.*
12. *Slice bananas and fold into the mixture.*
13. *Divide the mixture between the prepared pie crusts.*
14. *Garnish as desired and serve.*

BUTTERMILK PIE

Makes 2 servings

Ingredients:

2 bottom crusts, store-bought or see recipe page 95

1/3 cup granulated sugar

1/3 cup light brown sugar, packed

2 tablespoons unsalted butter, melted

1/2 teaspoon pure vanilla extract

1/4 cup buttermilk

1/3 cup heavy whipping cream

4 large egg yolks

Method:

1. Lay a foil strip over each pie mold to aid with removal once baked.
2. Cut out 2 bottom pie crusts using the large side of the pastry cutter.
3. Place bottom crusts over the foil strips into the pie molds then gently ease in by lifting the edges and pressing the centers.
4. Press the top edge of each crust into the grooved perimeter.
5. In a bowl, combine remaining ingredients; whisk until smooth.
6. Divide mixture evenly between the pie molds until almost full; close and latch the lid.
7. Plug in the pie maker and bake for 12-15 minutes or until the filling has set but is still wobbly.
8. When baking is complete, lift the pies by the foil strips to remove from the pie maker.
9. Let cool to room temperature, garnish as desired and serve.

CHOCOLATE
MOUSSE PIE

Makes 2 servings

Ingredients:

2 bottom chocolate pie crusts (see recipe on page 97)
1 3/4 cups heavy cream, divided
6 ounces bittersweet chocolate chips
2 tablespoons powdered sugar
1/2 cup hazelnuts, toasted

Method:

1. *Lay foil strips over each pie mold to aid with removal once baked.*
2. *Cut out bottom crusts using the large side of the pastry cutter.*
3. *Place bottom crusts over the foil strips into the pie mold then gently ease in by lifting the edges and pressing the centers; close and latch the lid.*
4. *Plug in the pie maker and bake crusts only for 12 minutes or until firm to the touch.*
5. *When baking is complete, lift the crusts by the foil strip to remove from the pie maker; let cool.*
6. *In a saucepan over medium heat, bring 3/4 cup of cream to a simmer.*
7. *Remove from heat then add the chocolate chips.*
8. *Let stand for 3 minutes then whisk until smooth; let cool to room temperature.*
9. *In a bowl, beat the remaining cream and sugar using a hand mixer until stiff peaks form.*
10. *Using a spatula, gently fold in the chocolate mixture until combined.*
11. *Divide the mixture between the 2 baked chocolate crusts.*
12. *Refrigerate pies for about 1 1/2 hours or until set.*
13. *Top with hazelnuts and serve.*

COCONUT CREAM PIE

Makes 2 servings

Ingredients:

2 bottom crusts, store-bought or see recipe on page 95

1 1/2 cups whole milk

1/3 cup granulated sugar

2 tablespoons all purpose flour

Pinch of kosher salt

2 egg yolks, slightly beaten

1 tablespoon unsalted butter

1/2 teaspoon vanilla

1/4 teaspoon coconut extract

1/2 cup coconut flakes, toasted

Method:

1. *Cut out 2 bottom pie crusts using the large side of the pastry cutter.*
2. *Lay a foil strip over each pie mold to aid with removal once baked.*
3. *Place bottom crusts over foil strips into the pie molds then gently ease in by lifting the edges and pressing the centers.*
4. *Press the top edge of each crust into the grooved perimeter; close and latch the lid.*
5. *Plug in the pie maker and bake crusts only for about 12 minutes or until desired doneness.*
6. *When baking is complete, lift crusts by the foil strips to remove from the pie maker; set aside.*
7. *In a large saucepan over medium heat, scald the milk.*
8. *In another saucepan over medium heat, combine the sugar, flour and salt; gradually stir in the scalded milk and cook until thickened, stirring constantly.*
9. *Cover and cook for an additional 2 minutes, stirring occasionally.*
10. *In a small bowl, have the slightly beaten egg yolks ready.*
11. *Stir a small amount of the hot mixture into the egg yolks; when combined, stir yolk mixture back into the remaining hot mixture.*
12. *Cook for an additional 1 minute, stirring constantly.*
13. *Remove from heat then blend in the butter, vanilla, coconut extract, and all but 2 tablespoons of coconut flakes.*
14. *Let cool until lukewarm then pour mixture into the prepared crusts.*
15. *Garnish with coconut flakes or as desired before serving.*

MISSISSIPPI
MUD PIE

Makes 2 servings

Ingredients:

2 bottom chocolate pie crusts (see recipe page 97)
3 tablespoons cocoa powder
1/3 cup light brown sugar, packed
1/3 cup cornstarch
Pinch of kosher salt
1 1/3 cups whole milk
1/4 teaspoon butter vanilla extract
1 teaspoon vanilla extract
1 tablespoon unsalted butter
Toasted pecans, chopped
Mini marshmallows

Method:

1. *Lay a foil strip over each pie mold to aid with removal once baked.*
2. *Cut out 2 bottom pie crusts using the large side of the pastry cutter.*
3. *Place bottom crusts over foil strips into the pie molds then gently ease in by lifting the edges and pressing the centers; close and latch the lid.*
4. *Plug in the pie maker and bake crusts only for 12 minutes or until firm to the touch.*
5. *When baking is complete, lift the crusts by the foil strips to remove from the pie maker; let cool.*
6. *In a large glass bowl, whisk together the cocoa, sugar, cornstarch, salt, milk and extracts; whisk well to dissolve the sugar and cocoa.*
7. *Microwave for 3 minutes then whisk again.*
8. *Continue to microwave for 2 minutes then whisk and repeat until mixture is thick, smooth and very bubbly.*
9. *Remove and whisk in the butter; cover and let cool until warm.*
10. *When mixture is warm, divide between the pie crusts.*
11. *Smooth the tops then garnish with pecans and marshmallows or as desired before serving.*

PEACH
PIE

Makes 2 servings

Ingredients:

4 cups fresh peaches, sliced

1/4 cup granulated sugar

2 tablespoons cornstarch

2 bottom pie crusts, store-bought or see recipe on page 95

2 top crusts, cut from store-bought puff pastry

Any decorative pie crust pieces, if desired

Method:

1. *In a 4-quart saucepan over medium-high heat, combine the peaches, sugar and cornstarch.*
2. *Cook for 10-12 minutes, stirring almost constantly, or until completely bubbly and thickened.*
3. *Boil for an additional 1 minute then remove from heat; stir mixture often as it cools.*
4. *Lay a foil strip over each pie mold to aid with removal once baked.*
5. *Cut out top and bottom pie crusts using the pastry cutter.*
6. *Place bottom crusts over foil strips into the pie molds then gently ease in by lifting the edges and pressing the centers.*
7. *Press the top edge of each crust into the grooved perimeter.*
8. *Spoon filling in each pie mold until slightly mounded above the rim.*
9. *Cover with top crusts and any decorative pie crust piece if desired; close and latch the lid.*
10. *Plug in the pie maker and bake for 12-15 minutes or until well browned.*
11. *When baking is complete, lift the pies by the foil strips to remove from the pie maker.*
12. *Garnish as desired and serve warm.*

BLUEBERRY PIE

Makes 2 servings

Ingredients:

4 cups fresh blueberries

1/4 cup granulated sugar

2 tablespoons cornstarch

2 bottom pie crusts, store-bought or see recipe on page 95

2 top pie crusts, cut from store-bought puff pastry

Any decorative pie crust pieces, if desired

Method:

1. *In a 4-quart saucepan over medium-high heat, combine the blueberries, sugar and cornstarch; stir well.*
2. *Cook for 10-12 minutes, stirring almost constantly, or until completely bubbly and thickened.*
3. *Boil for an additional minute then remove from heat; stir mixture often as it cools.*
4. *Lay a foil strip over each pie mold to aid with removal once baked.*
5. *Cut out top and bottom pie crusts using the pastry cutter.*
6. *Place bottom crusts over foil strips into the pie molds then gently ease in by lifting the edges and pressing the centers.*
7. *Press the top edge of each crust into the grooved perimeter.*
8. *Spoon filling into each pie mold until slightly mounded above the rim.*
9. *Cover with top crusts and any decorative pie crust pieces if desired; close and latch the lid.*
10. *Plug in the pie maker and bake for 12-15 minutes or until well browned.*
11. *When baking is complete, lift the pies by the foil strips to remove from the pie maker.*
12. *Garnish as desired and serve warm.*

HOMEMADE
CHERRY PIE

Makes 2 servings

Ingredients:

4 cups tart fresh cherries, pitted
1/4 cup granulated sugar
2 tablespoons cornstarch
2 bottom crusts, store-bought or see recipe on page 95
2 top crusts, cut from store-bought puff pastry

Method:

1. *In a 4-quart saucepan over medium-high heat, combine the cherries, sugar and cornstarch; stir well.*
2. *Cook for 10-12 minutes while stirring constantly, or until completely boiling and thickened.*
3. *Continue boiling for 1 minute then remove from heat and stir mixture often until cooled.*
4. *Lay a foil strip over each pie mold to aid with removal once baked.*
5. *Cut out top and bottom pie crusts using the pastry cutter.*
6. *Place bottom crusts over the foil strips into the pie molds then gently ease in by lifting the edges and pressing the centers.*
7. *Press the top edge of each crust into the grooved perimeter.*
8. *Spoon filling into each pie mold until slightly mounded above the rim.*
9. *Cover with a top crusts; close and latch the lid.*
10. *Plug in the pie maker and bake for 12-15 minutes or until well browned.*
11. *When bake is complete, lift the pies by the foil strips to remove from the pie maker.*
12. *Garnish as desired and serve warm.*

TIP

You can make this into peach pie or blueberry pie by substituting 3 cups of either blueberries or 3 cups fresh diced peaches keeping all the remaining ingredients the same.

KEY LIME
PIE

Makes 2 servings

Ingredients:

2 bottom crusts, store-bought or use recipe on page 95

1 can (14 ounces) sweetened condensed milk

4 large eggs

1 tablespoon fresh lime zest

1/2 cup fresh lime juice

Swiss Meringue Topping (see recipe on page 100)

Method:

1. *Cut out 2 bottom pie crusts using the large side of the pastry cutter.*
2. *Lay a foil strip over each pie mold to aid with removal once baked.*
3. *In a large bowl, combine the milk, eggs, lime zest and juice; mix until smooth using a hand mixer.*
4. *Place bottom crusts over the foil strips into the pie molds then gently ease in by lifting the edges and pressing the centers.*
5. *Press the top edge of each crust into the grooved perimeter.*
6. *Pour the milk mixture into each pie mold until 3/4 full; close and latch the lid.*
7. *Plug in the pie maker and bake for 12-15 minutes or until custard is set.*
8. *When baking is complete, lift the pies by the foil strips to remove from the pie maker.*
9. *Prepare the Swiss Meringue then pile on top of each pie into decorative swirls.*
10. *Preheat the oven to 500°F.*
11. *Place pies on a cookie sheet and bake for a few minutes until edges are browned (watch closely so they don't burn).*
12. *Garnish as desired and serve.*

NOT YOUR GRANDMA'S
APPLE PIE

Makes 2 servings

Ingredients:

2 large Granny Smith apples
2 Pink Lady or Golden Delicious apples
2 tablespoons unsalted butter
1/3 cup granulated sugar
1 teaspoon cinnamon
1/8 teaspoon ground allspice
Pinch of grated nutmeg
2 tablespoons cornstarch
2 bottom crusts, store-bought or see recipe page 95
2 top crusts, cut from store-bought puff pastry
Any pie crust decorations (optional)
Vanilla ice cream, for serving

Method:

1. *Peel, core and dice the apples into 1/2-inch cubes.*
2. *Preheat a large skillet over medium-high heat.*
3. *Add the butter to the skillet; when melted, add the sugar.*
4. *Stir until sugar begins to caramelize and turns amber in color.*
5. *Add the apples all at once; stir for a few minutes until apples begin to release some of their juice.*
6. *Add the cinnamon, allspice, nutmeg and cornstarch then stir until thickened and very bubbly.*
7. *Remove from heat and let cool.*
8. *Lay a foil strip over each pie mold to aid with removal once baked.*
9. *Cut out top and bottom crusts using the pastry cutter.*
10. *Place bottom crusts over foil strips into the pie molds then gently ease in by lifting the edges and pressing the centers.*
11. *Press the top edge of each crust into the grooved perimeter.*
12. *Pour about 1 cup of apple mixture into each pie mold until mixture mounds slightly above the rim.*
13. *Cover with a top crusts and any decorations if desired; close and latch the lid.*
14. *Plug in the pie maker and cook for 15 minutes or until well browned.*
15. *When cooking is complete, lift the pies by the foil strips to remove from the pie maker.*
16. *Serve with ice cream if desired.*

WHOOPIE PIE

Makes 6 Servings

Ingredients:

1 cup buttermilk
2 large eggs
1/3 cup unsalted butter, melted
2 teaspoons vanilla extract
3/4 cup granulated sugar
1 cup unbleached all purpose flour
1/2 cup good quality cocoa (see source page 106)
1/2 teaspoon baking soda
1/2 teaspoon baking powder
1/2 teaspoon kosher salt
Swiss Meringue Topping (see recipe on page 100)
Powdered sugar, for dusting (optional)

Method:

NOTE: Timing is important in this recipe. The cakes should be made, cooled and split before starting the Swiss Meringue recipe for the filling.

1. *In a mixing bowl, blend together the buttermilk, eggs, butter and vanilla using a hand whisk.*
2. *Whisk in remaining ingredients, except Swiss Meringue and powdered sugar.*
3. *Lay a foil strip over each pie mold to aid with removal once baked.*
4. *Pour 4 tablespoons of batter each pie mold; close and latch the lid.*
5. *Plug in the pie maker and bake for 10-12 minutes or until a wooden pick inserted off-center comes out with just a few moist crumbs clinging to it (If pick has a streak of shiny batter on it, cook for a couple of minutes more).*
6. *When baking is complete, lift the pies by the foil strips to remove from the pie maker.*
7. *Repeat to make more whoopie pies if desired.*
8. *Let pies cool then split each pie in half.*
9. *Spoon or pipe a generous amount of Swiss Meringue onto the bottom pie halves then cover with top pie halves.*
10. *Dust tops lightly with powered sugar if desired and serve.*

PEANUT BUTTER
PIE

Makes 2 servings

Ingredients:

2 bottom chocolate crusts (see recipe on page 97)
8 ounces unsalted butter
1 cup powdered sugar
1 cup peanut butter
1/2 teaspoon vanilla extract
1/4 teaspoon butter vanilla
1 large egg white, beaten to soft peaks
1 tablespoon salted peanuts (optional)

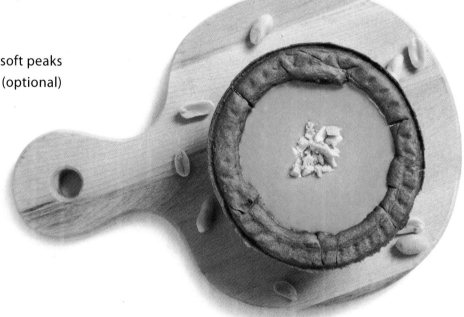

Method:

1. *Lay a foil strip over each pie mold to aid with removal once baked.*
2. *Cut out 2 bottom pie crusts using the large side of the pastry cutter.*
3. *Place bottom crusts over foil strips into the pie molds then gently ease in by lifting the edges and pressing the centers.*
4. *Press the top edge of each crust into the grooved perimeter; close and latch the lid.*
5. *Plug in the pie maker and bake crusts only for 12-15 minutes or until desired doneness.*
6. *When baking is complete, lift the crusts by the foil strips to remove from the pie maker; set aside.*
7. *In a bowl, combine the butter and sugar; mix using a hand mixer until light and fluffy.*
8. *Add the peanut butter and mix until smooth.*
9. *Add in the vanilla extract and butter vanilla; mix until combined.*
10. *Using a spatula, gently fold in the beaten egg white.*
11. *Divide the peanut butter filling between the prepared pie crusts.*
12. *Garnish with peanuts or as desired and serve.*

PECAN PIE

Makes 2 servings

Ingredients:

2 bottom crusts, store-bought or see recipe on page 95

2 large eggs

2 large egg yolks

2 tablespoon unsalted butter, melted

1 1/2 cups brown sugar, packed

2 teaspoons vanilla extract

1 cup toasted pecans, chopped

Method:

1. *Lay a foil strip over each pie mold to aid with removal once baked.*
2. *Cut out 2 bottom pie crusts using the large side of the pastry cutter.*
3. *Place bottom crusts over the foil strips into the pie molds then gently ease in by lifting the edges and pressing the centers.*
4. *Press the top edge of each crust into the grooved perimeter.*
5. *In a bowl, combine remaining ingredients; mix well.*
6. *Pour batter into each pie mold until 3/4 full; close and latch the lid.*
7. *Plug in the pie maker and bake for 15-20 minutes or until custard is set.*
8. *When baking is complete, lift the pies by the foil strips to remove from the pie maker; let cool.*
9. *Garnish as desired before serving.*

PUMPKIN PIE

Makes 2 servings

Ingredients:

2 bottom crusts, store-bought or use recipe on page 95
1 can (15 ounces) pumpkin puree
3/4 cup granulated sugar
1 tablespoon molasses
2 large eggs
1/4 teaspoon kosher salt
1 teaspoon vanilla extract
1/2 teaspoon grated nutmeg
1 teaspoon ground ginger
1/2 teaspoon ground cinnamon
Zest from 1/4 of a brightly skinned orange
1 1/2 cups heavy cream

Method:

1. *Cut out 2 bottom pie crusts using the large side of the pastry cutter.*
2. *In a bowl, combine remaining ingredients; mix well using a hand mixer.*
3. *Lay a foil strip over each pie mold to aid with removal once baked.*
4. *Place bottom crusts over foil strips into the pie molds then gently ease in by lifting the edges and pressing the centers.*
5. *Press the top edge of each crust into the grooved perimeter.*
6. *Pour pumpkin mixture into each pie mold until 2/3 full; close and latch the lid.*
7. *Plug in the pie maker and bake for 15-20 minutes or until filling is set.*
8. *When baking is complete, lift the pies by the foil strips to remove from the pie maker; let cool.*
9. *Garnish as desired and serve.*

STRABERRY
PIE

Makes 2 servings

Ingredients:

2 bottom crusts, store-bought or see recipe page 95
4 tablespoons cream cheese, softened
1 tablespoon powdered sugar
1 pint fresh strawberries
2 tablespoons seedless strawberry jam
Ice cream or whipped cream for serving (optional)

Method:

1. *Lay a foil strip over each pie mold to aid with removal once baked.*
2. *Cut out 2 bottom pie crusts using the large side of the pastry cutter.*
3. *Place bottom crusts over foil strips into the pie molds then gently ease in by lifting the edges and pressing the centers.*
4. *Press the top edge of each crust into the grooved perimeter.*
5. *Close and latch the lid; bake crust only for about 12 minutes or until desired doneness.*
6. *When baking is complete, lift the crusts by the foil strips to remove from the pie maker; set aside.*
7. *In a small bowl stir together the cream cheese and powdered sugar until smooth.*
8. *Divide mixture between the baked crusts.*
9. *If strawberries are large, cut in half or quarters.*
10. *Top each pie with strawberries.*
11. *In a small glass bowl, microwave the jam for 20 seconds to warm.*
12. *Stir then drizzle over the tops of the strawberries to add flavor and shine.*
13. *Garnish as desired and serve.*

TIP

You can use this same recipe and make it with any fruit that tastes good raw and that has a matching jam or jelly to go with it. Raspberries are my favorite but peaches and blueberries are very nice too. When fruit is fresh and ripe this is one of the best ways to show it off.

GRASSHOPPER TARTS

Makes 2 servings

Ingredients:

2 bottom chocolate crusts, see recipe on page 97

3/4 cup heavy cream

1/2 teaspoon vanilla extract

3 tablespoons powdered sugar

2 tablespoons crème de menthe liqueur

1/8 teaspoon peppermint extract

3 tablespoons white chocolate chips, melted until smooth

Chocolate curls (optional)

Method:

1. *Lay a foil strip over each pie mold to aid with removal once baked.*
2. *Cut out 2 bottom pie crusts using the large side of the pastry cutter.*
3. *Place bottom crusts over foil strips into the pie molds then gently ease in by lifting the edges and pressing the centers; close and latch the lid.*
4. *Plug in the pie maker and bake crusts only for 12 minutes or until firm to the touch.*
5. *When baking is complete, lift the crusts by the foil strips to remove from the pie maker; let cool.*
6. *In a bowl, whip the cream to stiff peaks using a hand whisk or hand mixer.*
7. *Whisk in the vanilla, powdered sugar, crème de menthe, peppermint extract and melted white chocolate; mix just until smooth.*
8. *Divide the mixture between the cooled tart shells.*
9. *Chill for 30 minutes then garnish with chocolate curls if desired and serve cold.*

TIP
Sometimes I line the bottom of the baked tart shells with chocolate mints and garnish the top with them as well.

FRESH BERRY TARTS

Makes 2 servings

Ingredients:

2 bottom crusts, store-bought or see recipe on page 95
1/2 cup fresh strawberries, sliced
1/2 cup fresh raspberries
1/2 cup fresh blueberries
1/2 cup fresh blackberries
2 teaspoons granulated sugar (optional)
Whipped cream for garnish (optional)

Method:

1. *Cut out 2 bottom pie crusts using the large side of the pastry cutter.*
2. *Lay a foil strip over each pie mold to aid with removal once baked.*
3. *Place bottom crusts over foil strips into the pie molds then gently ease in by lifting the edges and pressing the centers.*
4. *Press the top edge of each crust into the grooved perimeter; close and latch the lid.*
5. *Plug in the pie maker and bake crusts only for 12-15 minutes or until desired doneness.*
6. *When baking is complete, lift the crusts by the foil strips to remove from the pie maker.*
7. *Divide the berries between the prepared crusts.*
8. *Top each tart with 1 teaspoon of sugar if desired then garnish as desired and serve.*

ICE CREAM SUNDAE
TARTS

Makes 2 servings

Ingredients:

2 bottom chocolate crusts (see recipe on page 97)
Store-bought fudge ripple ice cream
Chocolate Ganache (see recipe on page 101)

Method:

1. *Lay a foil strip over each pie mold to aid with removal once baked.*
2. *Cut out 2 bottom pie crusts using the large side of the pastry cutter.*
3. *Place bottom crusts over foil strips into the pie molds then gently ease in by lifting the edges and pressing the centers.*
4. *Press the top edge of each crust into the grooved perimeter.*
5. *Close and latch the lid; bake crust only for about 12 minutes or until desired doneness.*
6. *When baking is complete, lift the crusts by the foil strips to remove from the pie maker; let cool.*
7. *Add desired amounts of ice cream scoops into each cooled crust.*
8. *Microwave ganache for a few seconds to soften.*
9. *Stir ganache until smooth and pourable.*
10. *Serve tarts with ganache.*

SORBET SUNDAE TARTS

Makes 2 servings

Ingredients:

2 bottom crusts, store-bought or see recipe on page 95
Store-bought sorbet

Method:

1. *Lay a foil strip over each pie mold to aid with removal once baked.*
2. *Cut out 2 bottom crusts using the large side of the pastry cutter.*
3. *Place bottom crusts over foil strips into the pie molds then gently ease in by lifting the edges and pressing the centers.*
4. *Press the top edge of each crust into the grooved perimeter.*
5. *Close and latch the lid; bake crust only for about 12 minutes or until desired doneness.*
6. *When baking is complete, lift the crusts by the foil strips to remove from the pie maker; let cool.*
7. *Add desired amounts of sorbet scoops to each crust.*
8. *Serve immediately.*

LEMON TART WITH MELON RIBBONS

Makes 2 servings

Ingredients:

2 bottom crusts, store-bought or see recipe on page 95
1 recipe Lemon Curd (see recipe on page 102)
1 wedge honeydew melon
1 wedge cantaloupe

Method:

1. *Lay a foil strip over each pie mold to aid with removal once baked.*
2. *Place bottom crusts over foil strips into the pie molds then gently ease in by lifting the edges and pressing the centers.*
3. *Press the top edge of each crust into the grooved perimeter; close and latch the lid.*
4. *Plug in the pie maker and bake crusts only for 12-15 minutes or until desired doneness.*
5. *When baking is complete, lift the pies by the foil strips to remove from the pie maker.*
6. *Fill each crust with lemon curd until 1/4-inch below the tart's top.*
7. *Use a mandoline slicer or vegetable peeler to slice long and thin "ribbons" from the melons.*
8. *Roll up each ribbon into a coil then arrange on top of lemon curd, peel-side up.*
9. *Serve tarts within 2 hours or the pastry will get soggy.*

TIP
You can also make beautiful ribbons out of mango, plums, peaches or pears.

3-2-1 QUICK FIX CAKE

Makes 1 cake with extra mix for later use

Ingredients:

1 box (16 ounces) angel food cake mix
1 box (15.25 ounces) other cake mix (any flavor)
2 tablespoons water

Method:

1. *In a large mixing bowl, whisk together both dry cake mixes until combined (do not add water, eggs or oil as suggested on the packaging).*
2. *Transfer the dry mix to a tall canning jar or other storage container until ready to use.*
3. *To make a quick-fix cake, combine 3 tablespoons of the dry mix and 2 tablespoons of cold water in a small bowl; stir to combine.*
4. *Lay a foil strip over the pie mold to aid with removal once baked.*
5. *Pour the batter into a single pie mold of the pie maker; close and latch the lid.*
6. *Plug in the pie maker and bake for 6 minutes or until the top of the cake springs back when pressed slightly.*
7. *When baking is complete, lift the cake by the foil strip to remove from the pie maker.*
8. *Serve immediately.*

TIP

This cake mix is perfect to have on hand for those sneaky sweet cravings. The mix will keep for months and it's really easy to make since you only have to add water. If you just remember 3-2-1 (3 tablespoons dry mix, 2 tablespoons water, 1 cake is what it makes) you won't even need a recipe to remember.

TANGERINE
TARTS

Makes 2 servings

For the Crusts:

2 bottom crusts, store-bought or see recipe page 95

For Topping:

Fresh or canned tangerine segments

For the Filling:

2 large egg yolks

7 ounces (from a 14 ounce can) sweetened condensed milk

1 tablespoon tangerine zest

2 tablespoons fresh tangerine juice

1 tablespoon fresh lemon juice

Method:

1. *Lay a foil strip over each pie mold to aid with removal once baked.*
2. *Cut out 2 bottom pie crusts using the large side of the pastry cutter.*
3. *Place bottom crusts over foil strips into the pie molds then gently ease in by lifting the edges and pressing the centers.*
4. *Press the top edge of each crust into the grooved perimeter.*
5. *In a bowl whisk together all filling ingredients.*
6. *Divide filling between the pie molds until almost full; close and latch the lid.*
7. *Plug in the pie maker and bake for 12-15 minutes or until filling is wobbly.*
8. *When baking is complete, lift the tarts by the foil strips to remove from the pie maker.*
9. *Arrange tangerine segments on top before serving.*

MOLTEN CHOCOLATE
LAVA CAKES

Makes 6 cakes

For the Cakes:

1 cup good quality cocoa powder (see source page 106)
2 cups unbleached all purpose flour
1 teaspoon baking powder
1/2 teaspoon baking soda
1 teaspoon kosher salt
3/4 cup unsalted butter, softened
2 cups granulated sugar
3 large eggs
2 teaspoons vanilla extract
1 1/2 cups whole milk

For the Lava Filling:

3/4 cup heavy whipping cream
1 1/2 cups semi-sweet chocolate pieces

Method:

1. *In a bowl, whisk together the cocoa, flour, baking powder, baking soda and salt; set aside.*

2. *In a bowl, cream together the butter and sugar using a mixer until fluffy.*

3. *Add the eggs and vanilla; beat until smooth then scrape the bowl.*

4. *Add the milk and the cocoa mixture; mix until smooth.*

5. *To make the lava filling, microwave the cream in a microwave-safe bowl until it boils.*

6. *Remove then add the chocolate to the hot cream; stir until the chocolate is melted; chill completely.*

7. *Lay a foil strip over each pie mold to aid with removal once baked.*

8. *Pour batter into each pie mold until 2/3 full.*

9. *Quickly spoon 2 tablespoons of very cold lava filling in the center of the cake batter in each pie mold then cover with some additional cake batter; close and latch the lid.*

10. *Plug in the pie maker and bake for 8 minutes then immediately unplug the pie maker and let rest for 10 minutes.*

11. *Lift the cakes by the foil strips to remove from the pie maker.*

12. *Garnish as desired and serve immediately (be careful as the lava filling is very hot and turned liquid during baking) and repeat with remaining batter if desired.*

VANILLA ANGEL
FOOD CAKE

Makes 2 servings

Ingredients:

1/2 cup cake flour
1/3 cup granulated sugar
6 large egg whites
1 1/2 teaspoons warm water
Pinch of kosher salt
1/4 teaspoon cream of tartar
1/3 cup additional granulated sugar
1 teaspoon vanilla extract
Swiss Meringue Topping (see recipe on page 100)
Lemon Curd (see recipe on page 102)

Method:

1. *Sift the flour and 1/3 cup granulated sugar together into a bowl; repeat once more to lighten.*
2. *In a clean bowl of stand mixer fitted with clean beaters, combine the egg whites, water, salt and cream of tartar; beat on medium speed until foamy.*
3. *Turn speed to medium-high and begin beating in the remaining 3/4 cup of sugar gradually and beat for 3-5 minutes or until soft peaks form (tips of the meringue should curl over).*
4. *Quickly beat in the vanilla then remove bowl from mixer.*
5. *Gently fold the flour mixture over the meringue mixture and fold to combine completely.*
6. *Add cupcake liners to the pie molds if desired.*
7. *Pour batter into the pie molds until 2/3 full; apply nonstick spray to the top of the pie maker.*
8. *Close and latch the lid then plug in the pie maker.*
9. *Bake for 12-15 minutes or until a wooden pick inserted off-center comes out clean.*
10. *Remove and let cool.*
11. *Once cooled, split the cake in half horizontally.*
12. *Place 2 tablespoons of lemon curd in the center of each cake then replace the tops.*
13. *Use a spoon to make a decorative design with the meringue and serve.*

STRAWBERRY CREAM CHEESE MINIS

Serves 2 servings

Ingredients:

6 large strawberries, stemmed
4 ounces cream cheese, softened
3 tablespoons granulated sugar
1 1/3 cups half & half
4 large egg yolks
1 large egg
2 bottom crusts, store-bought or see recipe page 95
Additional fresh berries for serving

Method:

1. *In a blender, combine the strawberries, cream cheese and sugar; purée until smooth.*
2. *Add the half & half, yolks and egg to the blender and purée for 5 seconds.*
3. *Lay a foil strip over each pie mold to aid with removal once baked.*
4. *Cut out 2 bottom crusts using the large side of the pastry cutter.*
5. *Place bottom crusts over foil strips into the pie molds then gently ease in by lifting the edges and pressing the centers.*
6. *Press the top edge of each crust into the grooved perimeter.*
7. *Divide strawberry mixture between the pie molds until almost full; close and latch the lid.*
8. *Plug in the pie maker and bake for 15-20 minutes or until centers are just wobbly.*
9. *When baking is complete, lift the pies by the foil strips to remove from the pie maker.*
10. *Chill for 1 hour then garnish with additional berries before serving.*

BROWNIE CUPS WITH PRETZELS

Makes 4 servings

Ingredients:

1/4 cup unsalted butter
4 ounces semi-sweet chocolate pieces
1 teaspoon vanilla extract
3/4 cup granulated sugar
2 large eggs
1/4 teaspoon kosher salt
1/2 cup all purpose flour
1/2 cup small salted pretzels

Method:

1. *In a large microwave-safe bowl, combine the butter and chocolate.*
2. *Microwave for 1 minute then stir until chocolate has completely melted.*
3. *Whisk in the vanilla and sugar until blended thoroughly.*
4. *Whisk in the eggs, salt and flour; mix just until all of the flour is mixed in.*
5. *Lay a foil strip over each pie mold to aid with removal once baked.*
6. *Add cupcake liners to the pie molds if desired.*
7. *Add a few pretzels to each pie mold then fill pie molds with brownie batter until 3/4 full.*
8. *Press several pretzels onto the brownie batter; close and latch the lid.*
9. *Plug in the pie maker and bake for 15-20 minutes or until a wooden pick inserted off-center comes out with just a few moist crumbs clinging to it (if there is a streak of shiny batter on the pick, continue baking for a few additional minutes).*
10. *When baking is complete, lift the brownie cups by the foil strips to remove from the pie maker.*
11. *Let cool before serving.*

BLACKBERRY CROISSANT
BREAD PUDDING

Makes 2-4 servings

Ingredients:

1 cup heavy cream

3 large eggs

1/3 cup granulated sugar

Pinch of kosher salt

1/2 teaspoon fresh lemon juice

1/2 teaspoon vanilla extract

3/4 cup fresh or frozen blackberries

3 day-old croissants, cut into 1/2-inch pieces

Whipped cream

Method:

1. *In a bowl, combine all ingredients, except croissants and whipped cream; mix well.*
2. *Lay a foil strip over each pie mold to aid with removal once baked.*
3. *Fill each pie mold with croissant pieces until 3/4 full.*
4. *Pour the cream mixture into each pie mold until it reaches the top of the croissants; close and latch the lid.*
5. *Plug in the pie maker and bake for 15-20 minutes or until set.*
6. *When baking is complete, lift bread pudding by the foil strips to remove from the pie maker.*
7. *Top with whipped cream before serving.*

TIP
You can make this
recipe with berries of
your choice.

63

CINNAMON ROLLS

Makes about 8 rolls

For the Rolls:

1 envelope active dry yeast

1/4 cup lukewarm water

1/2 cup whole milk

4 large eggs

4 cups unbleached all purpose flour, divided

1/3 cup granulated sugar

1/2 cup unsalted butter, softened

1 teaspoon kosher salt

For the Filling:

4 tablespoons unsalted butter

2 teaspoons vanilla extract

1 cup light brown sugar, packed

1 tablespoon ground cinnamon

1/2 cup dark raisins

For the Glaze:

Vanilla Glaze (see recipe on page 65)

Method:

1. *Combine the yeast and water in a stand mixer fitted with the dough hook; let stand for 5 minutes then mix on low speed while adding the milk and eggs.*

2. *Add 1 cup of flour, mix on medium speed for 2 minutes then add 2 cups of flour, sugar, butter and salt. Continue mixing for 2 minutes then add remaining flour and mix for an additional 3 minutes until a smooth but sticky dough forms. Cover with a towel and let rise for 1 hour.*

3. *On a lightly floured surface, punch the dough down, knead it into a ball then flatten it into a thick rectangle; cover with a towel and let rise for 15 minutes.*

4. *In a bowl, combine all filling ingredients; mix well then set aside.*

5. *Pat the dough into a large rectangle, spread filling then roll it up and pinch the edges.*

6. *Cut the roll into 2-inch sections.*

7. *Place a cinnamon roll into each pie mold; close and latch the lid.*

8. *Plug in the pie maker and bake for 10-15 minutes or until well browned.*

9. *Top with vanilla glaze and serve.*

BLACK & WHITE CUPCAKES

Makes 6 servings

For the Cupcakes:

1 recipe of chocolate cupcake (see page 98)
1 recipe of vanilla cupcake (page 99)

For the Vanilla Glaze:

1 1/4 cups powdered sugar
2 tablespoons water
1/4 teaspoon pure vanilla extract

For the Chocolate Glaze:

4 ounces semi-sweet chocolate chips
3 tablespoons unsalted butter
3 tablespoons whole milk
1 1/2 cups powdered sugar

Method:

1. *Lay a foil strip over each pie mold to aid with removal once baked.*
2. *Fill a squeeze bottle with chocolate cupcake batter until 3/4 full*
3. *Fill another squeeze bottle with vanilla cupcake batter until 3/4 full.*
4. *Squeeze both batters at the same into each pie mold until 3/4 full (hold squeeze bottles still while filling the pie molds); close and latch the lid.*
5. *Plug in the pie maker and bake for 12-15 minutes or until a wooden pick inserted off-center comes out clean.*
6. *When baking is complete, lift the cupcakes by the foil strips to remove from the pie maker and set aside to cool.*
7. *Repeat to make more cupcakes (the batters will keep in the refrigerator for up to 3 days or in the freezer for up to 3 months).*
8. *To make the chocolate glaze, combine the chocolate chips and butter in a microwave-safe bowl; microwave until melted.*
9. *Stir until smooth then stir in remaining chocolate glaze ingredients.*
10. *Keep covered until ready to use.*
11. *To make the vanilla glaze, combine all vanilla glaze ingredients and stir until smooth.*
12. *Top cupcakes with glazes before serving.*

CARROT CAKE CUPCAKES

Makes 4 servings

For the Cake:

2 large eggs
1/2 cup canola oil
1 1/3 cups granulated sugar
1 cup carrot, pureed
1/2 cup pineapple, pureed
1 1/2 teaspoons kosher salt
1 tablespoon ground cinnamon
2 cups unbleached all purpose flour
1 teaspoon baking soda
1 teaspoon baking powder
2 teaspoons vanilla extract

For the Icing:

1 1/2 cups powdered sugar
1/4 cup cream cheese, softened
2 tablespoons unsalted butter, soft
1/2 teaspoon vanilla extract

Method:

1. *In a large bowl, combine all cake ingredients; mix well.*
2. *Lay a foil strip over each pie mold to aid with removal once baked.*
3. *Pour batter into each pie mold until 3/4 full; close and latch the lid.*
4. *Plug in the pie maker and bake for 12-15 minutes or until a wooden pick inserted off-center comes out clean.*
5. *When baking is complete, lift the cupcakes by the foil strips to remove from the pie maker; let cool and repeat to make additional cupcakes if desired.*
6. *In a bowl, combine all icing ingredients; stir to combine then spread over the cupcakes.*
7. *Garnish as desired and serve (see fondant carrot instructions on page 105).*

GERMAN CHOCOLATE CUPCAKES

Makes 6 servings

For the Cupcakes:

1 recipe chocolate cupcakes (see recipe on page 98)

For the Pecan Coconut Icing:

1 cup pecan pieces, toasted

2 cups sweetened coconut flakes, toasted

1/4 cup unsalted butter

1/2 cup heavy cream

1 cup brown sugar, packed

1/2 teaspoon vanilla extract

1/8 teaspoon kosher salt

Method:

1. *Prepare the chocolate cupcake recipe.*
2. *To make the icing, combine all icing ingredients in a saucepan over medium-high heat; bring to a boil.*
3. *Let boil for 1 minute then remove from heat and let filling cool to room temperature.*
4. *Cut each cupcake in half horizontally then top bottom half with icing and replace the top.*
5. *Top with additional icing before serving.*

TIP

Extra icing will keep in the refrigerator for up to 3 days or in the freezer for up to 3 months.

MINT CHOCOLATE CHIP
CUPCAKES

Makes 4 servings

For the Cupcakes:

1 recipe chocolate cupcakes (see page 98)

1 teaspoon pure mint extract

1/4 cup mini chocolate chips

For the Mint Cream Cheese Frosting:

1 cup unsalted butter, softened

12 ounces cream cheese, softened

1 pound powdered sugar

1/2 teaspoon vanilla extract

1/2 teaspoon pure mint extract

A few drops of green food coloring (optional)

Chocolate mint leaves for garnish (optional)

Method:

1. *Stir the mint extract and chocolate chips into the prepared chocolate cupcake batter.*

2. *Place cupcake liners into the pie molds if desired.*

3. *Pour batter into each pie mold until 2/3 full; close and latch the lid.*

4. *Plug in the pie maker and bake for 10-12 minutes or until tops spring back when pressed slightly.*

5. *Remove using a small spatula and let cool completely; repeat with remaining batter if desired.*

6. *To make the frosting, whip the butter in a bowl using a hand mixer until fluffy.*

7. *Add the cream cheese and mix until completely smooth; scrape the bowl.*

8. *Add the powdered sugar, extracts and food coloring if desired and mix until smooth.*

9. *Frost the tops of the cooled cupcakes and decorate with chocolate mint leaves if desired before serving.*

TIP

To make the chocolate leaves, select large, unblemished fresh mint leaves and make sure they are dry. Microwave 2 tablespoons of semi-sweet chocolate chips until just barely melted then stir until slightly warm. Use a small brush to paint a layer of chocolate onto the underside of each mint leaf; let cool and set. Peel off the mint leaves before using if desired.

RAINBOW
CUPCAKES

Makes up to 6 cupcakes

Ingredients:

1 recipe of vanilla cupcake (see recipe on page 99)
6 paste food coloring (purple, blue, green, yellow, orange and red)

Method:

1. *Prepare the vanilla cupcake recipe.*
2. *Divide the batter evenly between 6 bowls.*
3. *Make the following colors using the chart provided with the food coloring packaging: red, orange, yellow, green, blue and purple.*
4. *Add food coloring into each bowl of batter (use a different color for each bowl) until desired food coloring is achieved.*
5. *Stir the batter in each bowl using separate spoons.*
6. *Pour the batter from each bowl into separate squeeze bottles (or spoon the batters into the pie molds).*
7. *Layer the different colored batters into each pie mold until 3/4 full; close and latch the lid.*
8. *Plug in the pie maker and bake for 12-15 minutes or until a wooden pick inserted off-center comes out clean.*
9. *Remove and set aside; let cool.*
10. *Repeat to make more cupcakes if desired (batter will keep in the refrigerator for up to 3 days or in the freezer for up to 3 months).*

RED VELVET CUPCAKES

Makes 6 servings

Ingredients:

1/2 cup shortening
1 1/2 cups granulated sugar
2 large eggs
1/4 cup red food coloring
1 teaspoon vanilla extract
1 cup buttermilk
1 teaspoon apple cider vinegar
2 tablespoons good quality cocoa
1/2 teaspoon kosher salt
1 teaspoon baking soda
2 1/4 cups unbleached all purpose flour
Cream Cheese Icing (see recipe on page 101)

Method:

1. *In a large bowl, combine the shortening and sugar; cream using a hand mixer until fluffy.*
2. *Add the eggs to the bowl; beat for 1 minute then scrape the bowl.*
3. *Add the food coloring, vanilla, buttermilk and vinegar to the bowl; mix well then scrape the bowl.*
4. *In a separate bowl, combine remaining ingredients, except icing; stir.*
5. *Pour the egg mixture into the cocoa mixture; mix until smooth.*
6. *Place a cupcake liner into each pie mold if desired.*
7. *Pour the batter into each pie mold until 3/4 full; close and latch the lid.*
8. *Plug in the pie maker and bake for 12-15 minutes or until a wooden pick inserted off-center comes out clean.*
9. *Remove cupcakes using a small spatula then repeat to make more cupcakes if desired (batter will keep in the refrigerator for up to 3 days or in the freezer for up to 3 months).*
10. *Top with cream cheese icing before serving.*

S'MORES
CUPCAKES

Makes 4 servings

Ingredients:

1 recipe chocolate cupcakes (see page 98)
4 store-bought graham crackers, broken
1/3 cup heavy cream
1/2 cup semi-sweet chocolate chips
1 recipe Swiss Meringue Topping (see page 100)

Method:

1. *Prepare the chocolate cupcake recipe.*
2. *Place a cupcake liner into each pie mold if desired.*
3. *Scatter some graham cracker pieces into the bottom of each pie mold.*
4. *Pour cupcake batter into each pie mold until 2/3 full; close and latch the lid.*
5. *Plug in the pie maker and bake for 10-12 minutes or until a wooden pick inserted off-center comes out with just a few moist crumbs clinging to it (if it has a streak of shiny batter, bake for a few more minutes).*
6. *When baking is complete, remove cupcakes using a small spatula and let cool.*
7. *Repeat to make more cupcakes if desired.*
8. *Pour the heavy cream into a microwave-safe bowl; microwave until bubbly.*
9. *Stir in the chocolate chips until melted and smooth.*
10. *Using a spoon, carve out a 1-inch deep hole into the top of the cupcakes.*
11. *Fill holes with the chocolate mixture.*
12. *Make the Swiss Meringue and pipe or spoon onto cupcakes.*
13. *Dip cupcakes into remaining melted chocolate mixture before serving.*

TIP

If you are pressed for time, use chocolate cake mix for the cupcakes, a jar of chocolate fudge and marshmallow crème for the topping.

STRAWBERRY CUPCAKES

Makes 6 servings

For the Cupcakes:

1 recipe vanilla cupcakes (see page 99)
2 cups strawberries, finely diced + more for garnish

For the Strawberry Whipped Cream:

3/4 cup heavy cream
2 tablespoons powdered sugar
2 tablespoons strawberry puree

Method:

1. *Prepare the vanilla cupcake recipe.*
2. *Using a spatula, gently fold in the strawberries.*
3. *Place a cupcake liner into each pie mold if desired.*
4. *Pour batter into the pie molds until 3/4 full; close and latch the lid.*
5. *Plug in the pie maker and bake for 12-15 minutes or until a pick inserted off-center comes out clean.*
6. *Remove, set aside to cool and repeat to make more cupcakes if desired.*
7. *To make the whipped cream, beat the heavy cream and powdered sugar in a mixing bowl using a hand mixer until soft peaks form then gently fold in the strawberry puree using a spatula.*
8. *Top cupcakes with strawberry whipped cream, garnish as desired and serve.*

CHOCOLATE KISS
CUPCAKES

Makes 6 servings

For the Cupcakes:

1 cup good quality cocoa powder (see source page 106)

2 cups unbleached all purpose flour

1 teaspoon baking powder

1/2 teaspoon baking soda

1 teaspoon kosher salt

3/4 cup unsalted butter, softened

2 cups granulated sugar

3 large eggs

2 teaspoons vanilla extract

1 1/2 cups whole milk

Swiss Meringue Topping (see recipe on page 100)

For the Lava Filling:

3/4 cup heavy whipping cream

1 1/2 cups semi sweet chocolate pieces

Method:

1. *In a bowl, whisk together the cocoa, flour, baking powder, baking soda and salt; set aside.*

2. *In a separate bowl, cream together the butter and sugar using a mixer until fluffy.*

3. *Add the eggs and vanilla to the butter mixture and beat until smooth; scrape the bowl.*

4. *Add the milk and flour mixture; mix until smooth.*

5. *To make the lava filling, heat the cream in a microwave-safe bowl until it boils.*

6. *Remove then add the chocolate to the cream; stir until chocolate is melted then chill completely.*

7. *Add cupcake liners to the pie molds if desired.*

8. *Fill each pie mold with batter until 2/3 full.*

9. *Quickly spoon 2 tablespoons of very cold lava filling in the center of the cake batter in each pie mold then top with some additional batter; close and latch the lid.*

10. *Plug in the pie maker and bake for 8 minutes then unplug the pie maker immediately and let rest for 10 minutes.*

11. *Remove carefully using a small spatula (lava filling is hot).*

12. *Top with Swiss Meringue, garnish as desired and serve warm.*

CHOCOLATE MALTED
CUPCAKES

Makes 6 servings

Ingredients:

1 cup unsalted butter, softened

3 cups light brown sugar, packed

4 large eggs

1 tablespoon vanilla extract

2/3 cup good quality cocoa powder (see source page 106)

2 tablespoons malted milk powder

2 teaspoons baking soda

1/2 teaspoon kosher salt

2 cups cake flour

1 1/2 cups sour cream

1 1/3 cups water

1 cup malted milk balls, chopped and divided

Cream Cheese Icing (see recipe on page 101)

Method:

1. *In a bowl, combine the butter and sugar; cream using hand mixer until fluffy.*
2. *While mixing, add the eggs (one at a time) then add the vanilla and beat until smooth.*
3. *Sift the cocoa powder, malted milk powder, baking soda, salt and flour.*
4. *Slowly add flour mixture to the butter mixture, alternating with the sour cream and water until all ingredients have been added; mix until smooth.*
5. *Folding in 1/2 cup of the malted milk balls.*
6. *Add cupcake liners to the pie molds if desired.*
7. *Pour batter into the pie molds until 3/4 full; close and latch the lid.*
8. *Plug in the pie maker and bake for 10-12 minutes or until a wooden pick inserted off-center comes out clean.*
9. *Remove from pie maker using a spatula; let cool and repeat to make more cupcakes if desired.*
10. *Top cooled cupcakes with cream cheese icing then scatter some of the malted milk balls over the cupcakes before serving.*

CHOCOLATE ROSE CUPCAKES

Makes 6 servings

Ingredients:

1 cup unsalted butter, softened

3 cups light brown sugar, packed

4 large eggs

1 tablespoon vanilla extract

2/3 cup good quality cocoa powder (see source page 106)

2 teaspoons baking soda

1/2 teaspoon kosher salt

2 cups cake flour

1 1/2 cups sour cream

1 1/3 cups water

Chocolate Ganache (see recipe on page 101)

Method:

1. *In a bowl, combine the butter and sugar; cream using hand mixer until fluffy.*
2. *While mixing, add the eggs (one at a time) then add the vanilla and beat until smooth.*
3. *Sift the cocoa powder, baking soda, salt and flour.*
4. *Slowly add the flour mixture to the bowl, alternating with the sour cream and water until all ingredients have been added; mix until smooth.*
5. *Add cupcake liners to the pie molds if desired.*
6. *Pour batter into the pie molds until 3/4 full; close and latch the lid.*
7. *Plug in the pie maker and bake for 12-15 minutes or until a wooden pick inserted off-center comes out clean.*
8. *Remove from pie maker using a spatula; let cool and repeat to make more cupcakes if desired.*
9. *Swirl ganache decoratively onto each cupcake.*
10. *Top each with a fondant rose before serving (see fondant rose instructions on page 105).*

CHOCOLATE MOCHA
CUPCAKES

Makes 6 servings

For The Cupcakes:

1 cup unsalted butter, softened
3 cups light brown sugar, packed
4 large eggs
1 tablespoon vanilla extract
2/3 cup good quality cocoa powder
2 teaspoons baking soda
1/2 teaspoon kosher salt
2 cups cake flour
1 1/2 cups sour cream
1 1/3 cups water

For The Mocha Icing:

2 cups powdered sugar
1/2 cup unsalted butter, softened
1 teaspoon vanilla extract
2 teaspoons instant coffee granules
2 teaspoons hot water

Method:

1. *In a bowl, combine the butter and sugar; cream using hand mixer until fluffy.*
2. *While mixing, add the eggs (one at a time) then add the vanilla and beat until smooth.*
3. *Sift the cocoa powder, baking soda, salt and flour.*
4. *Slowly add flour mixture to the butter mixture, alternating with the sour cream and water until all ingredients have been added; mix until smooth.*
5. *Add cupcake liners to the pie molds if desired.*
6. *Pour the batter into the pie molds until 3/4 full; close and latch the lid.*
7. *Plug in the pie maker and bake for 10-12 minutes or until a wooden pick inserted off-center comes out clean.*
8. *Remove from pie maker using a spatula; let cool and repeat to make more cupcakes if desired.*
9. *To make the icing, combine the powdered sugar and butter in a bowl and beat using a hand mixer until fluffy.*
10. *Add the vanilla then stir the coffee granules into the hot water to dissolve before adding to the bowl; beat until fluffy.*
11. *Top cooled cupcakes with mocha icing, garnish as desired and serve.*

RASPBERRY CHARLOTTE CUPCAKES

Makes 6 servings

For The Cupcakes:

3 cups cake flour

1 1/2 cups all purpose flour

3/4 teaspoon baking soda

2 1/4 teaspoons baking powder

2 teaspoons kosher salt

1 cup + 2 tablespoons unsalted butter

2 1/3 cups granulated sugar

5 large eggs

3 large egg yolks

2 cups buttermilk

1 tablespoon vanilla extract

1/2 teaspoon butter-vanilla extract

For The Whipped Cream:

2 cups heavy cream

1/4 cup vanilla extract

1/3 cup powdered sugar

2 cups fresh raspberries

2 packages store-bought ladyfingers

Method:

1. *In a bowl, sift together the flours, baking soda, baking powder and salt.*
2. *In a separate bowl, combine the butter and sugar; cream using a hand mixer until fluffy.*
3. *While mixing on medium speed, add the eggs (one at a time) then add the egg yolks.*
4. *While mixing, add the flour mixture and buttermilk in batches, alternating between the two until incorporated.*
5. *Add the extracts and mix to incorporate.*
6. *Add cupcake liners to the pie molds if desired.*
7. *Pour batter into the pie molds until 3/4 full; close and latch the lid.*
8. *Plug in the pie maker and bake for 12-15 minutes or until a wooden pick inserted off-center comes out clean.*

9. *Remove using a small spatula; let cool and repeat to make more cupcakes if desired.*

10. *To make the whipped cream, in the bowl of a stand mixer fitted with the whisk attachment, combine the cream, vanilla and powdered sugar.*

11. *Whip on medium-high speed until stiff peaks form.*

12. *Place each cupcake on a serving plate and spoon enough whipped cream over to coat top and sides (it does not have to be neat).*

13. *Place ladyfingers vertically around each cupcake like a fence.*

14. *Wrap a ribbon around the ladyfingers to secure and tie into a pretty bow.*

15. *Fill center with raspberries until they are the height of the ladyfingers.*

16. *Garnish as desired and serve.*

CONFETTI

CUPCAKES

Makes 6-8 servings

Ingredients:

3 cups cake flour

1 1/2 cups all purpose flour

3/4 teaspoon baking soda

2 1/4 teaspoons baking powder

2 teaspoons kosher salt

1 cup + 2 tablespoons unsalted butter

2 1/3 cups granulated sugar

5 large eggs

3 large egg yolks

2 cups buttermilk

1/2 cup (2 ounces) pastel confetti sprinkles, divided

1 tablespoon vanilla extract

1/2 teaspoon butter-vanilla extract

Cream Cheese Icing (see recipe on page 101)

Method:

1. *In a bowl, sift together the flours, baking soda, baking powder and salt.*
2. *In a separate bowl, combine the butter and sugar; cream using a hand mixer until fluffy.*
3. *While mixing on medium speed, add the eggs (one at a time) then the egg yolks.*
4. *While mixing, add the flour mixture and buttermilk in batches, alternating between the two until incorporated then fold in 3 tablespoons of the sprinkles.*
5. *Add the extracts and mix to incorporate.*
6. *Add cupcake liners to the pie molds if desired.*
7. *Pour batter into the pie molds until 3/4 full; close and latch the lid.*
8. *Plug in the pie maker and bake for 12-15 minutes or until a wooden pick inserted off-center comes out clean.*
9. *Remove using a small spatula and let cool; repeat to make more cupcakes if desired.*
10. *Stir 2 tablespoons of the sprinkles into the prepared cream cheese icing.*
11. *Top cooled cupcakes with some icing and sprinkles, garnish as desired and serve.*

DULCE DE LECHE CUPCAKES

Makes 6 servings

Ingredients:

3 cups cake flour
1 1/2 cups all purpose flour
3/4 teaspoon baking soda
2 1/4 teaspoons baking powder
2 teaspoons kosher salt
1 cup + 2 tablespoons unsalted butter
2 1/3 cups granulated sugar
5 large eggs
3 large egg yolks
2 cups buttermilk
1 tablespoon vanilla extract
1/2 teaspoon butter-vanilla extract
Cream Cheese Icing (see recipe on page 101)
1 cup store-bought dulce de leche

Method:

1. *In a bowl, sift together the flours, baking soda, baking powder and salt.*
2. *In a separate bowl, combine the butter and sugar; cream using a hand mixer until fluffy.*
3. *While mixing on medium speed, add the eggs (one at a time) then add the egg yolks.*
4. *While mixing, add the flour mixture and buttermilk in batches, alternating between the two until incorporated.*
5. *Add the extracts and mix to incorporate.*
6. *Add cupcake liners to the pie molds if desired.*
7. *Pour batter into the pie molds until 3/4 full; close and latch the lid.*
8. *Plug in the pie maker and bake for 12-15 minutes or until a wooden pick inserted off-center comes out clean.*
9. *Remove using a small spatula and let cool; repeat to make more cupcakes if desired.*
10. *Top cooled cupcakes with some prepared cream cheese icing then spoon a generous amount of dulce de leche over the top of the icing before serving.*

SANDWICH COOKIE
CUPCAKES

Makes 6 servings

Ingredients:

3 cups cake flour

1 1/2 cups all purpose flour

3/4 teaspoon baking soda

2 1/4 teaspoons baking powder

2 teaspoons kosher salt

1 cup + 2 tablespoons unsalted butter

2 1/3 cups granulated sugar

5 large eggs

3 large egg yolks

2 cups buttermilk

1 tablespoon vanilla extract

1/2 teaspoon butter-vanilla extract

12 double stuffed chocolate sandwich cookies

Chocolate Ganache (see recipe on page 101)

Method:

1. *In a bowl, sift together the flours, baking soda, baking powder and salt.*
2. *In a separate bowl, combine the butter and sugar; cream using a hand mixer until fluffy.*
3. *While mixing on medium speed, add the eggs (one at a time) then add the egg yolks.*
4. *While mixing, add the flour mixture and buttermilk in batches, alternating between the two until incorporated.*
5. *Add the extracts and mix to incorporate.*
6. *Add cupcake liners to the pie molds if desired.*
7. *Pour 2 tablespoons of batter into each pie mold; close and latch the lid.*
8. *Plug in the pie maker and bake for about 4 minutes to "set" the batter.*
9. *Open the lid and place 2 sandwich cookies on top of batter in each pie mold.*
10. *Top with additional batter until pie molds are 3/4 full; close and latch the lid.*
11. *Bake for an additional 8-10 minutes or until well browned.*
12. *Remove using a small spatula; let cool and repeat to make additional cupcakes if desired.*
13. *Top cooled cupcakes with some ganache before serving.*

WORMS IN DIRT
CUPCAKES

Makes 6 servings

Ingredients:

1 cup unsalted butter, softened

3 cups light brown sugar, packed

4 large eggs

1 tablespoon vanilla extract

2/3 cup good quality cocoa powder (see source page 106)

2 teaspoons baking soda

1/2 teaspoon kosher salt

2 cups cake flour

1 1/2 cups sour cream

1 1/3 cups water

Chocolate Ganache (see recipe on page 101)

18 candy worms

Method:

1. *In a bowl, combine the butter and sugar; cream using hand mixer until fluffy.*
2. *While mixing, add the eggs (one at a time) then add the vanilla and beat until smooth.*
3. *Sift the cocoa powder, baking soda, salt and flour.*
4. *Slowly add the flour mixture to the butter mixture, alternating with the sour cream and water until all ingredients have been added; mix until smooth.*
5. *Add cupcake liners to the pie molds if desired.*
6. *Pour the batter into the pie molds until 3/4 full; close and latch the lid.*
7. *Plug in the pie maker and bake for 10-12 minutes or until a wooden pick inserted off-center comes out clean.*
8. *Remove using a small spatula; let cool and repeat to make more cupcakes if desired.*
9. *Take 1 of the cooled cupcakes and break it into small crumbs using your fingers. This will be the "dirt" part.*
10. *Ice remaining cupcakes with chocolate ganache.*
11. *Roll the iced top of each cupcake into the chocolate crumbs.*
12. *Top each cupcake with candy worms and serve.*

LEMON CHIFFON
FONDANT CUPCAKES

Makes 6 servings

Ingredients:

1 1/8 cup cake flour
3/4 cup granulated sugar
1/2 teaspoons kosher salt
1 1/2 teaspoons baking powder
1/4 cup canola oil
3 large egg yolks
1/4 cup water
1 tablespoon fresh lemon zest
2 tablespoons fresh lemon juice
3 large egg whites
1/8 teaspoon cream of tartar
Cream Cheese Icing (see recipe on page 101)
Easy Marshmallow Fondant (see page 104)

Method:

1. *In a large mixing bowl, sift together the flour, sugar, salt and baking powder.*
2. *In a separate bowl, whisk the oil, yolks, water, lemon zest and juice until light.*
3. *In a stand mixer fitted with the whip attachment, combine the egg whites and cream of tartar then mix on highest speed until very stiff peaks form and whites begin to lose their shine.*
4. *Remove from mixer then fold the flour mixture into the egg yolk mixture.*
5. *Fold the egg whites into the yolk/flour mixture using a spatula.*
6. *Add cupcake liners to the pie molds if desired.*
7. *Pour batter into each pie mold until 2/3 full; close and latch the lid.*
8. *Plug in the pie maker and bake for 10-12 minutes or until a wooden pick inserted off-center comes out with just a few moist crumbs clinging to it. If there is a streak of shiny batter, cook for a few additional minutes.*
9. *Remove using a small spatula; let cool completely and repeat to make more cupcakes if desired (or reserve batter for later use in the refrigerator for up to 3 days).*

10. *Invert completely cooled cupcakes onto serving plates, trimming tops (which will become bottoms) if necessary.*

11. *Apply a thin layer of cream cheese icing to the sides and top, it does not have to be perfect.*

12. *Cover cupcakes with the fondant as instructed on page 104 and garnish as desired.*

13. *Serve within one day.*

BLUE GELATIN STRIPED CUPCAKES

Makes 4 servings

Ingredients:

1 recipe vanilla cupcake (see recipe on page 99)
1 box (3.1 ounces) blue gelatin
1/2 cup boiling water

Method:

1. Prepare the vanilla cupcake recipe.
2. Let cupcakes cool completely.
3. Push a drinking straw about 3/4 of the way from the top into the cupcakes to make the holes.
4. Make about 5-6 holes into the top of each cupcake.
5. Place the gelatin in a mixing bowl and add the water; stir until dissolved.
6. Spoon the gelatin slowly into the holes of each cupcake.
7. Refrigerate cupcakes for 30 minutes.
8. Remove from refrigerator, garnish as desired and serve.

ALL AMERICAN
CUPCAKES

Makes 6 servings

For the Cupcakes:

1 recipe chocolate or vanilla cupcakes (see page 98 or 99)

For the Icing:

2 cups heavy cream

1/4 cup powdered sugar

1 teaspoon vanilla extract

Red and blue food coloring

Method:

1. *Prepare the chocolate or vanilla cupcake recipe.*
2. *In a bowl, combine the heavy cream, sugar and vanilla; whisk until combined.*
3. *Separate the icing into 3 equal portions in 3 separate bowls.*
4. *Don't add any food coloring to the bowl with the white icing.*
5. *Put 2-3 drops of red food coloring into the second bowl and stir icing until combined.*
6. *Put 2-3 drops of blue food coloring into the third bowl and stir icing until combined.*
7. *Place 3/4 cup of each color of icing into a small pastry bag.*
8. *Pipe the icing onto the cupcakes as shown in the picture.*
9. *Garnish as desired and serve.*

TIP

If you don't have pastry bags, a zip-type bag will work just fine. After you put the icing in the bag, use scissors and carefully cut off one of the corners to the desired size.

CHERRY TUNNEL CUPCAKES

Makes 6 servings

Ingredients:

1 recipe chocolate or vanilla cupcakes (see recipe on page 98 or 99)
3/4 cup store-bought cherry pie filling
Whipped topping

Method:

1. Prepare the chocolate or vanilla cupcake recipe.
2. Let cupcakes cool completely.
3. Using a melon baller, scoop out the center of the cupcakes from the top, making sure not to go all the way through.
4. Place 2 tablespoons of cherry pie filling into each cupcake.
5. Garnish with whipped topping and serve.

TIP
If you want to make this recipe even more special, use the filling recipe from the homemade cherry pie on page 44.

RECIPES

88

BAKED
ALASKA

Makes 2 servings

Ingredients:

1 recipe chocolate cupcake (see recipe on page 98)
2 scoops vanilla ice cream
Swiss Meringue Topping (see recipe on page 100)

Method:

1. *Prepare the chocolate cupcake recipe.*
2. *Place the ice cream scoops between 2 pieces of plastic wrap.*
3. *Using a small plate, flatten the ice cream to about 3/4-inch thick.*
4. *Cut a cupcake in half horizontally to form a top and bottom.*
5. *Put the ice cream in the middle then place on a small oven-safe plate.*
6. *Place this cupcake with the ice cream filling in the freezer for a minimum of 1 hour.*
7. *Prepare the meringue recipe.*
8. *Set oven to broil.*
9. *Put 2 cups of meringue into a pastry bag.*
10. *Remove the cupcake from the freezer and pipe meringue onto the cupcake in a decorative pattern.*
11. *Place the plate with the meringue-covered cupcake under the broiler for 1-2 minutes to brown the meringue.*
12. *Carefully remove from oven using an oven mitt and serve.*
13. *Repeat with remaining ingredients to make additional Baked Alaska desserts.*

GLUTEN-FREE BLUEBERRY MINI MUFFINS

Makes 4 servings

Ingredients:

2 cups buttermilk

2 large eggs

1/4 cup unsalted butter, melted

1/4 cup granulated sugar + more for topping

1 teaspoon vanilla extract

1 teaspoon kosher salt

1 teaspoon baking powder

1/2 teaspoon baking soda

1 1/4 cups cornstarch

1 1/4 cups potato starch

1/8 teaspoon xanthan gum

1 cup fresh blueberries

Method:

1. *In a bowl, combine all ingredients, except blueberries.*
2. *Gently fold in the blueberries right before baking.*
3. *Lay a foil strip over each pie mold to aid with removal once baked.*
4. *Add a cupcake liner to each pie mold if desired.*
5. *Fill each pie mold with batter until 3/4 full; close and latch the lid.*
6. *Plug in the pie maker and bake for 12-15 minutes or until golden brown.*
7. *When baking is complete, lift the muffins by the foil strips to remove from the pie maker.*
8. *Remove and dip top of muffins in sugar while still warm.*
9. *Repeat with remaining batter if desired and serve.*

GLUTEN-FREE CHOCOLATE CHIP MUFFINS

Makes 4 servings

Ingredients:

2 cups buttermilk

2 large eggs

1/4 cup unsalted butter, melted

1/4 cup granulated sugar + more for topping

1 teaspoon vanilla extract

1 teaspoon kosher salt

1 teaspoon baking powder

1/2 teaspoon baking soda

1 1/4 cups cornstarch

1 1/4 cups potato starch

1/8 teaspoon xanthan gum

1 cup semi-sweet of milk chocolate chips

Method:

1. *In a bowl, whisk together all ingredients, except chocolate chips.*
2. *Fold in the chocolate chips right before baking.*
3. *Add cupcake liners to the pie molds if desired.*
4. *Pour batter into the pie molds until 3/4 full; close and latch the lid.*
5. *Plug in the pie maker and bake for 12-15 minutes or until golden brown.*
6. *Remove using a spatula and repeat with remaining batter to make additional muffins.*

GLUTEN-FREE PEPPERONI PIZZA PIE

Makes 2 Pizzas

For the Crusts:

2 tablespoons olive oil

1 cup + 2 tablespoons water

1/3 cup dry potato flakes

1 cup white rice flour

1/2 cup tapioca flour

3 tablespoons powdered milk

1 teaspoon onion powder

1 teaspoon kosher salt

2 teaspoons xanthan gum

2 teaspoons unflavored gelatin

1 envelope dry active yeast

3 tablespoons dried egg whites

1 tablespoon granulated sugar

For the Filling:

4 tablespoons marinara sauce

1 cup mozzarella cheese, shredded

2 tablespoons Parmesan cheese, grated

8 ounces gluten-free pepperoni, sliced

Kosher salt and fresh pepper to taste

Method:

1. *Place all crust ingredients in order listed into a stand mixer fitted with the paddle attachment.*
2. *Mix dough on medium speed for 5 minutes, scraping the bowl if necessary.*
3. *Remove dough from mixer and let rest for 15 minutes.*
4. *On an oiled piece of plastic wrap, pat out the dough until 1/4-inch thick.*
5. *Cut out top and bottom crusts using the pastry cutter.*
6. *Lay a foil strip over each pie mold to aid with removal once baked.*
7. *Use the plastic wrap to support the fragile dough as you lift it.*

8. *Press the bottom crusts gently into the pie molds using your fingers and patching any tears that may have occurred.*

9. *Divide the filling ingredients in the order listed between the pie molds.*

10. *Cover with top crusts; close and latch the lid.*

11. *Plug in the pie maker and cook for 12-15 minutes or until browned.*

12. *When baking is complete, lift the pies by the foil strips to remove from the pie maker and serve immediately.*

TIP

To freeze extra dough, place dough balls into quart-size zip top bags. Spray the inside of the bags with nonstick spray before adding the dough balls. The dough will keep frozen for up to 2 months. When ready to use, thaw before using.

GLUTEN-FREE PIE CRUST

Makes about 4 bottom crusts and 4 top crusts

Ingredients:

1 cup unsalted butter, softened

8 ounces cream cheese, softened

1/2 teaspoon kosher salt

1 cup cornstarch

1 cup tapioca starch

1/2 teaspoon xanthan gum

1/2 teaspoon unflavored gelatin

Method:

1. *In a food processor, stand mixer or bowl with a hand mixer, combine all ingredients; mix until a dough ball forms.*

2. *Divide the dough into 2 portions then flatten into each into a round disk.*

3. *Wrap in plastic wrap and chill for 30 minutes or up to 3 days.*

4. *On a piece of plastic wrap lightly dusted with cornstarch, roll out the dough from the center to the outer edges until 1/8-inch thick.*

5. *Cut out pie crusts using the pastry cutter.*

6. *Repeat with the other dough and re-roll scraps to make more if desired.*

7. *Use the plastic wrap to support the fragile dough as you lift it.*

8. *Lay a foil strip over each pie mold to aid with removal once baked.*

9. *Press the bottom crusts gently into the pie molds using your fingers and patching any tears that may have occurred.*

10. *Proceed with desired filling and cover with top crusts if desired.*

11. *Plug in the pie maker and bake until desired doneness.*

TIP

For even more flavor, substitute the brown butter from page 103 for the unsalted butter.

BASIC PIE CRUST

Makes 4-6 bottom crusts + extra for decorating

Ingredients:

2 1/2 cups all purpose flour
1/2 teaspoon kosher salt
1/2 cup unsalted butter, cubed and cold
6 tablespoons shortening, cold
6 tablespoons ice water, divided

Method:

1. *Combine the flour, salt, butter and shortening in a food processor fitted with the S-blade.*
2. *Pulse until butter and shortening are the size of peas.*
3. *While pulsing, add 5 tablespoons water through the feed tube (if dough ball does not form in a few seconds, add remaining water).*
4. *Divide the dough ball into 2 portions then flatten into round disks.*
5. *Wrap in plastic wrap and chill for 30 minutes or for up to 3 days.*
6. *Unwrap a cold disk and place it on a lightly floured surface.*
7. *Roll out the dough from the center to the outer edges until 1/8-inch thick.*
8. *Cut out bottom pie crusts using the large side of the pastry cutter.*
9. *Cut out decorative pieces for tops such as lattice or leaves if desired.*
10. *Repeat with the other dough and re-roll scraps to make more if desired.*
11. *Store unused, cut pie dough crusts and decorations between sheets of parchment or plastic wrap, refrigerated for up to 3 days or frozen for up to 3 months.*

PHYLLO DOUGH

Makes 6 top crusts

Ingredients:

1/2 cup unsalted butter, melted
1 package (17.1 ounces) phyllo dough, thawed

Method:

1. *Place the butter into a tall drinking glass.*
2. *Unroll the phyllo dough and cover with a damp paper towel (trim any wet or stuck together edges from the dough using scissors to avoid tearing later).*
3. *Place 1 sheet of phyllo dough on the counter.*
4. *Dip a pastry brush into the butter (do not to let the brush touch the bottom of the glass where the milk solids are).*
5. *Drizzle the butter on the brush over the perimeter of the phyllo dough then lightly brush butter over the dough's surface (disregard some minor tears that may occur).*
6. *Place another sheet of phyllo dough on top and repeat with the butter.*
7. *Repeat until you have 6 sheets of layered phyllo dough and butter.*
8. *Reserve remaining phyllo dough for another use, it will keep refrigerated for a month.*
9. *Cut out 6 top pie crusts using the small side of the pastry cutter (press and twist cutter firmly to ensure that you're cutting through all dough layers).*
10. *Proceed with desired filling and bottom crusts then bake until desired doneness.*

TIP

If you want to make the bottoms out of phyllo crust, you can cut
2 bottom crusts from 6 more sheets of buttered and stacked phyllo dough.
This pastry is well worth using as it is delightfully crispy and flaky.

CHOCOLATE PIE
CRUST

Makes about 4 bottom pie crusts

Ingredients:

2 1/4 cups unbleached all purpose flour
1/2 teaspoon kosher salt
1/3 cup granulated sugar
1/2 cup good quality cocoa
1/2 cup unsalted butter, cold and cubed
3 large eggs

Method:

1. *Combine the flour, salt, sugar and cocoa in a food processor fitted with the S-blade.*
2. *Pulse to combine then add the butter and pulse until texture is mealy.*
3. *Add the eggs and pulse until a dough ball forms; remove dough.*
4. *Divide the dough ball into 2 portions then flatten each into a round disk.*
5. *Wrap in plastic wrap and chill for 30 minutes or for up to 3 days.*
6. *Unwrap a cold disk and place it on a lightly floured surface.*
7. *Sprinkle top of dough with flour then roll out the dough from the center to the outer edges until 1/8-inch thick.*
8. *Cut out the bottom pie crusts using the large side of the pastry cutter.*
9. *Repeat with the other dough and re-roll scraps to make more if desired.*
10. *Store unused, cut pie dough crusts and decorations between sheets of parchment or plastic wrap, refrigerated for up to 3 days or frozen for up to 3 months.*

DOUGHS & TOPPINGS

TIP
You can enhance the chocolate flavor of this crust by adding 2 teaspoons of instant espresso or coffee granules.

CHOCOLATE
CUPCAKES

Makes about 6 cupcakes

Ingredients:

1 cup unsalted butter, softened

3 cups light brown sugar, packed

4 large eggs

1 tablespoon vanilla extract

2/3 cup high quality cocoa powder

2 teaspoons baking soda

1/2 teaspoon kosher salt

2 cups cake flour

1 1/2 cups sour cream

1 1/3 cups water

Method:

1. *In a bowl, combine the butter and sugar; cream using a hand mixer until fluffy.*
2. *While mixing, add the eggs (one at a time) then add the vanilla and beat until smooth.*
3. *Sift the cocoa powder, baking soda, salt and flour then slowly add them to the bowl, alternating with the sour cream and water until all ingredients have been added; mix until smooth.*
4. *Save the batter for other cupcake recipes in this book or continue baking below.*
5. *Add cupcake liners to the pie molds if desired.*
6. *Pour batter into the pie molds until 3/4 full; close and latch the lid.*
7. *Plug in the pie maker and bake for 10-12 minutes or until a wooden pick inserted off-center comes out clean.*
8. *Remove from pie maker using a spatula; let cool and repeat to make more cupcakes if desired.*
9. *Top as desired and serve.*

TIP

The batter will keep in the refrigerator for up to 3 days and in the freezer for up to 3 months.

VANILLA CUPCAKES

Makes about 6 cupcakes

Ingredients:

3 cups cake flour
1 1/2 cups all purpose flour
3/4 teaspoon baking soda
2 1/4 teaspoons baking powder
2 teaspoons kosher salt
1 cup + 2 tablespoons unsalted butter
2 1/3 cups granulated sugar
5 large eggs
3 large egg yolks
2 cups buttermilk
1 tablespoon vanilla extract
1/2 teaspoon butter-vanilla extract

Method:

1. *In a bowl, sift together the flours, baking soda, baking powder and salt.*
2. *In a separate bowl, combine the butter and sugar; cream using a hand mixer until fluffy.*
3. *While mixing the butter mixture on medium speed, add the eggs (one at a time) then add the egg yolks.*
4. *While mixing, add the flour mixture and buttermilk in batches, alternating between the two until incorporated.*
5. *Add the extracts and mix to incorporate.*
6. *Save the batter for other cupcake recipes in this book or continue baking below.*
7. *Add cupcake liners to the pie molds if desired.*
8. *Pour batter into the pie molds until 3/4 full; close and latch the lid.*
9. *Plug in the pie maker and bake for 10-12 minutes or until a wooden pick inserted off-center comes out clean.*
10. *Remove from pie maker using a spatula; let cool and repeat to make more cupcakes if desired.*
11. *Top as desired and serve.*

TIP
If you are short on time, just use a box of cake mix.

SWISS MERINGUE
TOPPING

Makes enough for 4 small pies

Ingredients:

4 large egg whites
1 cup granulated sugar
1/2 teaspoon vanilla extract

Method:

1. *Wash hands, bowl, mixer whisks, anything that will come in contact with the egg whites as any form of grease, even a bit of egg yolk will inhibit the mixture from getting fluffy and stiff.*

2. *Whisk egg whites and sugar together in the top of a double boiler set over medium heat with 1-inch of simmering water in the bottom pot.*

3. *Whisk gently until all grains of sugar have dissolved and mixture is warm. Do not let mixture get too hot. This will take a few minutes.*

4. *Pour egg white mixture into bowl of stand mixer fitted with whisk attachment or use a hand mixer.*

5. *Beat mixture on highest speed until stiff peaks form (tips stand straight up). This will take several minutes.*

6. *Briefly beat in vanilla.*

7. *Mixture is only workable for about 8-10 minutes. After that time frame it "sets" and will look curdled and soft if piped or disturbed.*

8. *Mixture can be piped or spooned onto tart shells. Make decorative swirls or even spikes by lifting the spoon straight up from the surface of the meringue.*

TIP

For a baked meringue topping place tarts under the broiler until they brown, this will only take a few minutes, or, use a blowtorch for a fun and fast way to brown the meringue.

CREAM CHEESE ICING

Makes about 2 cups

Ingredients:

1/2 cup unsalted butter, softened
1/2 cup cream cheese, softened
1/2 teaspoon vanilla extract

1/2 teaspoon fresh lemon juice
4 cups powdered sugar, sifted

Method:

1. *In a stand mixer fitted with the paddle attachment, combine the butter and cream cheese.*
2. *Mix for 3-5 minutes or until smooth.*
3. *Scrape down the mixer then mix for an additional 1 minute.*
4. *Add remaining ingredients and mix on low speed until just blended and smooth; do not over mix.*
5. *Use icing on your favorite cupcakes or store covered and refrigerated for up to 5 days.*

CHOCOLATE GANACHE

Makes about 2 1/2 cups

Ingredients:

1 1/4 cups heavy whipping cream
3 cups good quality semi-sweet chocolate chips

Method:

1. *Pour the whipping cream into a large microwave-safe bowl.*
2. *Microwave for about 4 minutes to bring the cream to a simmer.*
3. *Remove then carefully pour the chocolate chips into the hot cream; let stand for 1 minute.*
4. *Whisk until smooth and shiny (mixture thickens as it cools).*
5. *You can use it warm and pour it over a cake to make a very shiny and smooth coating, or chill slightly to create a more fudgy consistency.*
6. *Ganache can be kept refrigerated for up to 2 weeks.*

LEMON CURD

Makes about 3 cups

Ingredients:

2 cups water
3/4 cup granulated sugar
2 tablespoons lemon zest + 2 teaspoons lemon zest
3/4 cup fresh lemon juice
6 large egg yolks
3/4 cup unsalted butter, cubed

Method:

1. *Fashion a double boiler out of a saucepan and a glass or stainless steel mixing bowl that will nest inside the saucepan with about half of it sticking above the rim.*

2. *Pour the water into the saucepan then place the mixing bowl on top.*

3. *Combine all remaining ingredients, except butter and 2 teaspoons lemon zest, into the bowl; whisk slowly.*

4. *Set heat to medium-high and stir gently for 5-8 minutes or until mixture is too hot to touch and has thickened significantly.*

5. *Pass the mixture through a fine strainer; let cool for 5 minutes.*

6. *Whisk in the butter until melted and smooth.*

7. *Whisk in remaining lemon zest.*

8. *Store airtight in the refrigerator for up to 2 weeks or freeze for up to 2 months.*

BROWN BUTTER

Makes about 1 cup

Ingredients:

1 1/2 cups (3 sticks) unsalted butter

Method:

1. *Bring the butter to a simmer in a sauté pan over medium heat. The butter will foam so use a spoon to push foam away so you can monitor color.*

2. *After a few minutes, butter will stop foaming and begin to turn a very light amber color.*

3. *Continue simmering until butter smells delightfully nutty and color turns to a medium amber with small flecks of darker brown in bottom of pan.*

4. *Immediately remove from heat then pour it into a wide heat-proof bowl. This is important because it stops the cooking process and prevents you from burning the butter.*

5. *Let cool and store refrigerated in an airtight container for up to 3 months.*

DOUGHS & TOPPINGS

EASY MARSHMALLOW
FONDANT

Makes about 2 pounds

Ingredients:

2 bags (10.5 ounces each) mini marshmallows

2 tablespoons water

1/3 cup shortening

1/2 teaspoon butter vanilla extract or clear vanilla (optional)

2 pounds powdered sugar, sifted

Cornstarch, as needed for rolling and kneading

Food coloring (if desired)

Method:

1. *In a large microwave-safe bowl, combine the marshmallows, water, shortening and vanilla if desired.*

2. *Microwave for 2 minutes, remove and stir.*

3. *Microwave again for 2 minutes and stir until the marshmallows are melted and smooth.*

4. *Pour the mixture into the bowl of a stand mixer fitted with the paddle attachment.*

5. *Add the powdered sugar then set the mixer to low speed; mix until incorporated, scraping the sides if necessary.*

6. *Carefully transfer the hot fondant mixture onto a very clean counter dusted with cornstarch.*

7. *Knead the mixture into a smooth ball (knead in the food coloring if desired).*

8. *Before applying to a dessert, heat in the microwave for 30 seconds to facilitate rolling.*

9. *Roll out using cornstarch (use a silicone mat and rolling pin for best results).*

10. *Store any unused fondant in an airtight container for up to 1 month at room temperature.*

To decorate cupcakes, color fondant as desired and roll out warmed fondant on a cornstarch dusted surface. To cover cupcake completely with fondant, roll out a 8-inch circle, 1/8-inch thick. Drape over cold cupcake and use your hands to press fondant against the cupcake, lifting up any pleats that form and easing the fondant onto the cupcake. Use a pizza cutter to cut away excess fondant. Use a pizza cutter or pastry wheel to cut shapes and designs. Cookie cutters are also great for shapes. Mold small pieces into petals for flowers such as roses or into little strawberries using the holes on a box grater to add texture and simulate the strawberry seeds. Brushing a cupcake with a bit of jam, such as apricot helps the fondant stick to the sides of the cupcake.

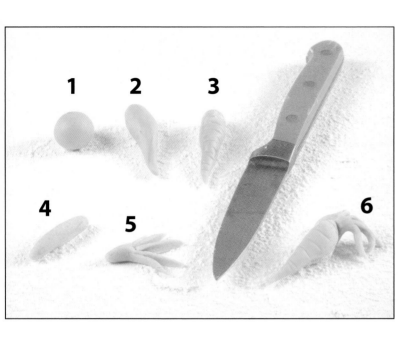

To Make a Fondant Carrot:

Step 1: **Roll orange fondant into a small ball**

Step 2: **Roll ball into a teardrop**

Step 3: **Cut lines into the carrot using a paring knife**

Step 4: **Roll green fondant into an oval shape**

Step 5: **Use a paring knife to partially cut stands into the oval**

Step 6: **Attach green strands to the carrot with a dot of water**

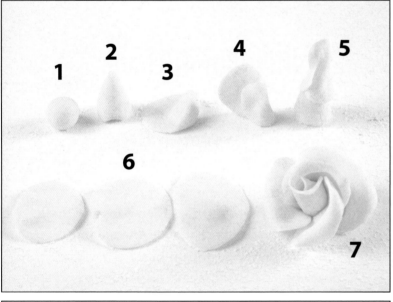

To Make a Fondant Rose:

Step 1: **Roll pink fondant into small balls**

Step 2: **Press 1 ball into a "kiss" shape**

Step 3: **Flatten one side of another ball**

Step 4: **Begin to roll up the ball from step 3**

Step 5: **To make the rose center, attach the rolled up ball to the "kiss" shaped ball from step 2 by pressing the sides**

Step 6: **Flatten one side of several more balls similar to step 3 in different sizes from small to large**

Step 7: **Attach the petals in concentric rows around the rose center by pressing the sides**

Step 8: **Roll out green fondant and cut out leaf shapes then cut lines into the fondant using a paring knife so it resembles a leaf**

Step 9: **Assemble rose with leaves**

SOURCE PAGE

Here are some of my favorite places to find ingredients that are not readily available at grocery stores as well as kitchen tools and supplies that help you become a better cook.

Chocosphere

P.O. Box 2237
Tualatin, OR 97062
877-992-4623

Excellent quality cocoa (Callebaut)
All Chocolates
Jimmies and sprinkles
www.chocosphere.com

D & G Occasions

625 Herndon Ave.
Orlando, FL 32803
407-894-4458

My favorite butter vanilla extract by Magic Line, cake and candy making supplies, citric acid, pure fruit oils, professional food colorings, ultra thin flexible spatulas, large selection of sprinkles and jimmies, unusual birthday candles, pure vanilla extract, pastry bags and tips, parchment, off-set spatulas, oven and candy thermometers, kitchen timers
www.dandgoccasions.com

Fortune Products, Inc.

205 Hickory Creek Road
Marble Falls, TX 78654
830-693-6111

Inexpensive, hand-held Accusharp knife sharpeners
www.accusharp.com

Rolling Pin Kitchen Emporium

P.O. Box 21798
Long Beach, CA 90801
949-221-9399

Cheesecloth, inexpensive "harp" shaped vegetable peelers, measuring cups and spoons, knives, vast array of kitchen tools including microplane graters, blow torches, baking pans and dishes, silicone pastry/cookie cutters
www.rollingpin.com

Penzeys Spices

P.O. Box 924
Brookfield, WI 53045
800-741-7787

Spices, extracts, seasonings and more
www.penzeys.com

Nui Enterprises

501 Chapala St. Suite A
Santa Barbara, CA 93101
805-965-5153

Vanilla beans from Tahiti and pure
vanilla extract
www.vanillafromtahiti.com

Whole Foods

550 Bowie St.
Austin, TX 78703
512-477-4455

Grains, citric acid, natural and organic
products, xanthan gum, gluten-free
baking items, real truffle oil, miso paste
www.wholefoods.com

Gluten Free Mall

4927 Sonoma HWY Suite C1
Santa Rosa, CA 95409
707-509-4528

All ingredients needed for gluten-free baking
www.glutenfreemall.com

The Bakers Catalogue at King Arthur Flour

135 Route 5 South
P.O. Box 1010
Norwich, VT 05055

Pure fruit oils, citric acid, silicone spatulas,
digital timers, oven thermometers, real truffle
oil, off-set spatulas, measuring cups and
spoons, knives, ice cream scoops, cheesecloth,
microplane graters, cookie sheets, baking pans
www.kingarthurflour.com

INDEX

FOR ALL OF MARIAN GETZ'S COOKBOOKS AS WELL AS COOKWARE, APPLIANCES, CUTLERY AND KITCHEN ACCESSORIES BY WOLFGANG PUCK

PLEASE VISIT HSN.COM
(KEYWORD: WOLFGANG PUCK)